The Untold Story

William Hershel Nelson

ATHENA PRESS
6 656 290 000

The Untold Story
Copyright © William Hershel Nelson 2009

All Rights Reserved

No part of this book may be reproduced in any form
by photocopying or by any electronic or mechanical means,
including information storage or retrieval systems,
without permission in writing from both the copyright
owner and the publisher of this book.

ISBN: 978 1 84748 703 2

First published 2007 by
DN Publications Ltd

Second edition published 2009 by
ATHENA PRESS
Queen's House, 2 Holly Road
Twickenham TW1 4EG
United Kingdom

Printed for Athena Press

The Untold Story

Dedication

This book is dedicated to my family and friends, and to the brave soldiers who fought by my side.

Acknowledgements

I would like to thank my grandson Daniel and family friend Sheridan Basten for their kind efforts in helping me to create and publish this book. Without their hard work and ongoing support this story would have remained untold.

Contents

INTRODUCTION	9
PART ONE: The Early Years	11
Childhood in Maine	13
Teenage Years	35
PART TWO: Man at War	53
Conscription	55
The D-Day Landings	76
Front-line Action	103
Digging In	128
Wounding, Marriage and the Postal Unit in Japan	156
The Eye of the Storm	187
PART THREE: A New Life in England	217
Coming Home	219
A Growing Family	240
EPILOGUE	267

Introduction

Many hours I have sat and wondered, where do I start my story? I realised it has to go back to my earliest childhood memories. It is not a work of fiction but a truthful account of my life, as far as it is possible for me to remember. It will also be a reminder of the hardships and the joys that my family and I experienced together.

At eighty-four years of age I want to hand down something of my life's journey to my family here and in America.

It was a great sadness to me that my own father never told me his life story. I am sure it would have been very interesting.

PART ONE:
The Early Years

Childhood in Maine

I was born on the 27 January 1924, the coldest night of that year. The temperature dropped to thirty below zero and the cooking range had to have wood burning into it all night long to maintain a degree of warmth. This did not mean the whole building was warm; there was no central heating, so the rest of the house was cold. To counteract this, everybody had to wear more clothes and go to bed with what they had on. I was born on my mother's birthday, which made me a special present for my mum. I do not know how much pain my poor mother went through giving me life but anyway I am sure she and Dad loved me very much, even though it meant another mouth to feed. So the Nelson family increased to seven.

There were only three homes that I can remember in my childhood. The first house I knew very little about, for this old building was where the first of the clan was born. It was said that this house was haunted. Every night ghosts were seen often walking through doors and walls, making loud groaning sounds. I was only told this in later years but I had never seen a ghost or spectre and so found it hard to believe this was why the family had moved away from the very old building. However, there must have been many a fond memory of my brothers Vincent, John Jr and Ralph, my favourite, with my sisters Stella, Freda and Thelma, who were all brought up in the large old field house with an upstairs attic where they slept.

All of the family mentioned above were brought into the world with the kind help of a neighbour. Doctors were very hard to find and too expensive for most families and so nearly ninety per cent of babies were born without midwives. This was the main reason why so many women died during childbirth. Anyway, the hospitals were very rare places and were spread many miles apart from each other.

My mother and one of my sisters were known to be mediums and more often than not a group of people would gather around the circular brown-stained table, clasping each others hands and talking to the spirits. It was not unusual for some of the folks of Camden to turn up and have their fortunes told, after paying for a cup of Mum's delicious tea. I've been told she was very good at reading the tea leaves. Sadly, everything had to end. Dad was getting fed up with the crowd of townsfolk and so decided to move from the field house.

A week later, all the family helped to pack up and move to a new place where ghosts didn't exist. This second house was where I was born. The home my dad chose was at the top of a road called Sand Street. It was a very large building with views of outstanding beauty that once seen could never be forgotten. Standing outside the front door and looking straight in front, one could see a well-worn dirt pathway, then a makeshift bridge over the slow-running brook. This entered the outskirts of the huge graveyard that lay a short distance away.

No one could miss seeing the slight rise in the ground revealing another part of the huge graveyard. Above this stood large, towering pine trees with their long, green needles and pine cones glistening in the sun. All of these were at the foot of the mountain. Then above this bit of greenery, when the autumn came, the maple leaves turned nearly all colours of the rainbow. It was a sight I shall never forget.

I should mention here that my father built this house. He owned in the region of twenty-five acres of land but half of it was woodland. The land was acquired on a small holding basis – registration of a Claim to Land. The land was practically worthless, but not if you could use the wood to build your own home and use a plot for vegetables.

The house had no running water, but just on the left a pathway led to the water well. Whenever water was needed, two pails were used to collect it. Even to this day, I believe it was the best beverage one could drink and it certainly quenched a person's thirst. The house had a large kitchen with a black iron cooking range with a twelve-inch black stovepipe running up and out of the roof of the attic where all us children slept. Downstairs was a lounge-cum-kitchen and a bedroom for our parents. It had a very large wooden outhouse attached to the kitchen where a toilet was situated. The toilet could not be flushed because of the lack of running water, thus it was a hole dug five feet deep with a frame of wood on top with a toilet seat to sit on and it had an old door that was attached to it for privacy.

The very long dirt road came to an abrupt end just outside the front of our home and to the left of my parents' home, an old man and his dog lived. He was a very nice neighbour but unfortunately he suffered from epilepsy. Everyone felt sorry for him but there was no cure for this type of condition.

At the top of the road and in front of the house, a pathway led over a brook of slowly running water, to lead into the bottom part of a very large cemetery. Here one could see lots of family history etched on the gravestones. As one looked toward the stones, one saw a huge, solitary pine tree and it was here where Mum's father and her sister, Goldie, were buried. Later in life we were told that they had chosen this as their final resting place because of its great beauty. The graveyard also faced other houses. These were just beside our own house which was the last house situated at the top of Sand Street.

I have already mentioned that I was the first child in the Nelson family to have been born in this building and, of course, I was lucky, for I left all the ghosts behind to haunt the old field house without me. I'm sure Mum missed her talks with the 'other world' but, of course, time moves on, and anyway, her life was interrupted by the arrival of yours truly, and now instead of six there were seven children to bring up.

When I got older, my father took me aside and told me it had been such a cold wicked night that Mum and he were afraid that I would not survive it. He cuddled me and said, 'When I looked down at your small face, I had the feeling that my little boy was a real fighter and would beat all the odds.' And he was right!

The beginning of this childhood story was told to me as I grew older, but I have retained certain memories.

At about two years old I encountered an old man wearing a black bowler hat. He smiled at me, picked me up and held me in his arms for a short time, then kissed me on the forehead and put me back on the ground. Then the dog Rex, who lived next door, licked my face when he saw me. I tried to follow the man as he left, but being only two, I could not keep up with him. My mother always seemed to be in the right place every time, so she carried me back to the house and very gently lay me on a chair and I remember seeing her wave to the old man as he left. It was only later in life that I found out it had been my mother's father who cuddled me ever so gently.

At an early age, I began to take more notice of what I saw, but sometimes events happened that confused me. One such very odd event occurred when I did not see my brother Vincent and sister Stella for a whole week. It really upset me, for they always picked me up and played hide and seek with me, and so I went crying to Mother. She held me in her arms, stroking my head and laughingly told me, 'Buddy, God has united them in marriage, so they may be away for some time.' Of course, I did see them occasionally, but I didn't know what the word marriage meant. I soon forgot about it, for other things kept my young mind busy.

Between four and five years old, I was at the age when a youngster tries to do things he sees his parents do. This, of course, made me do things that could have killed me. Firstly, I tried to go to the outer toilet instead of the old brass potty, after my mum had told me never to use the outside toilet on my own. I very slowly crept out of the back door and made for the toilet. It was not totally shut and so I was able to open it but held my breath for it made a scraping noise and I waited a while in case Mum turned up. I took my trousers down but it was a bit of a job to climb on to the toilet. Eventually, I was able to stand above the open hole cut in the middle. I did not try sitting on the hole for it was too large and so I straddled it. I bet you know what happened next; for down into the stinking hole I fell, yelling as I did so. If my arms had not been outstretched then I would not be here today.

My mum had heard me yell and was on the scene in no time. Good old Mum, I reckon she should have worn a gas mask, but she pulled me out of the hole and everyone available had to take pail after pail to the water well to pour over me. To be quite honest, I very nearly drowned and the smell lingered for hours. We occasionally had a skunk fall into the hole, and it would be interesting to know how he got out, but God knows he always left the smell behind.

The subject of outside toilets brings me to another memory. The old man who lived next door to us had a very large vegetable garden next to my dad's and once a year he would take a big home-made wheelbarrow and work for about four hours, shovelling all the human manure out of the hole in his toilet and into his wheelbarrow and, passing our home, take it to his own vegetable garden. On one occasion, Mum had to take us out for the day, for the smell was so vile. I must admit, he had some of the best vegetables for miles around.

To return to my youthful misadventures, I was always interested in how everything worked and this curiosity could have killed me, too. Our home had a long flight of steep stairs going up to a landing. A yard away from the top step, hanging from the ceiling, was a flowered shade, but the light bulb had blown. I had been close to my father many times when he changed the bulb and I thought how easy it looked. I remember one day, I pulled out a chair from beside one of the beds in the attic, put it just under the light and somehow got on to it. I had to stand up and look above me to reach the bulb holder but luckily I pulled it out, and holding it in one hand, I somehow got off the chair and searched for another bulb. To my delight, I found a spare one in a nearby chest of drawers and also saw an old knife lying beside it, which I put into my small ragged pocket.

Why, I do not know.

Going back to the chair, I was again able to climb on to it. Noticing where the old bulb came out, I tried to push the new one into the vacant hole but it would not go into it. So, I took the knife from my pocket, I pushed it into the empty round hole and then there sounded a very loud bang, followed by a bright flash of light. I suppose you could say I was a very lucky boy to be alive, for I just tumbled off the chair, rolled down the steps of the stairs and into my mother's arms. Good old Mum, she was always there in times of need and by golly I certainly needed her then. My dad never spanked me for doing this stupid thing but had a long talk with me about electricity and how I should respect it. It was a lesson well learnt and to this day I have never fooled around with electrical sockets.

Every so often, my mother did some sewing for a neighbour just down the road. She didn't make much money out of her work but every little helped and on this particular day she left me on my own. I wandered off down Sand Street to arrive at the old schoolhouse. Wearing no shoes, I walked up to the door to give it a thump with the sole of my foot. I waited a while and, when no one came, I banged on the door again. The door opened and there stood a very old stern-looking lady.

She looked down at me with disbelief on her face and smiled.

'What have we here?' she asked as she took me by the arm.

'Please, I want to see my sister,' I replied.

'And so you shall my young man,' she said.

Then she led me into the building, taking me to where Thelma sat, and put me into a seat beside her. Thelma looked at me with dismay. My face was dirty, my hair was not combed and I looked a real mess. At four years old I had no idea how my sister felt and everyone was giggling at her discomfort. After a short time Mrs Gould came over and said, 'I do believe your young brother has come to school without your mother's knowledge, so it would be quite all right if you took him home and returned to the classroom tomorrow.'

The teacher escorted the two of us to the door and waved goodbye to me as I left. Even today I can still see the smile on her face. My sister took me by the hand and we both hurried home to see our distraught mother, who had been looking for me. There were tears in her eyes as she raised me up for a cuddle. This was not the end of my trip to school for when my dad got home from work he spanked my bum and then pointed his finger at me saying, 'Don't ever do that again.' Although my backside was quite sore, I did not know what I had done wrong.

It's surprising how quickly time went by for, in no time, I had turned five and this meant I had to go to kindergarten. My mum packed me up a couple of sandwiches and on the first day went with me to the brand new schoolhouse near the town. Telling me to take heed where we were going as she would only take me there for a few days, after which I would have to go to school on my own. The first day it was just wonderful. There was one thing I was happy about – I knew the class teacher well, for her name was Mrs Gould. We played all types of games and we got to know each other.

I did feel sorry for some of my new friends as they did nothing but cry, but, the next day they were dry-eyed and took some interest in the new counting games. I felt very proud of myself and three days later even walked to school on my own. I climbed a tree on the way, I suppose to show off, but got the front of my clean shirt dirty.

One week into school I became ill, and although we could not afford to call the doctor, my mother and neighbour knew what to do. They put me straight to bed in a darkened room, for both of them agreed I was suffering from the measles. God, I did feel sick and the longer I lay the worse I felt. I knew very little about sickness at my young age; Mum told me a long time later they had expected me not to live but against all odds I survived and about three weeks later I was on my way to the classroom again and eager to see my school chums.

My first year at school went quickly and I found that I became teased about different things, mainly because of the way I was dressed. Not having new clothes like most of the others made me feel different and a bit of a loner. I got quite used to the teasing as time went by, but many times showed my feelings with my fists.

I always had a few lovely home-cut sandwiches from the bread Mum baked and at first I had a small bottle of milk to drink as well, but this soon stopped for there weren't any cows outside in the cold winter. Therefore, milk became too expensive and so in the end we only had about two bits of bread, sometimes with peanut butter. I remember the hardship we children went through and God knows how all the family survived. A good meal after getting home from school was rare, for it would always depend on what was in the cellar. I can remember leaving school one day and coming to the path through the cemetery. There was a cornfield and it wasn't unknown for me to pick a cob off a dead plant and eat it. Even though it tasted like sawdust, it was filling.

Then the long winter arrived and in November the snow began to fall. All night long it came, leaving snowdrifts four feet high. The next morning, my sister Annie (who was two years younger than me) and I looked out of the attic window upstairs and saw the landscape outside covered completely in the whiteness of snow. It was a really beautiful sight and just looking at it made us feel very cold.

Annie and I watched Dad open the downstairs window, climb out of it and shovel the drift away from the front door, so my mother could open it. My sister pulled up the window to see Dad more closely and moved aside to let me look as well.

Both of us leaned out too far and as Annie fell she grabbed my shirt and down we went together. Dad looked up and stood aside as my sister screamed. Where did we land? Well, luckily in the large snow bank my father had shovelled away from the outside door. God was surely with us that day, for the snow broke our fall and everyone looked at each other in amazement. As our mum opened the door we all three broke out laughing while she looked on in astonishment. Although we had a good laugh, we both were scolded and I do believe we learnt our lesson.

It was very cold that morning as Dad left for work with his black dinner pail tucked under his arms. He pointed at the two of us, smiled and said, 'I do hope this will teach you to behave yourselves,' and he left us, walking very slowly in the icy snow.

The winter snow got higher and higher, just the right depth for a reindeer to pull his sleigh. It was the night before Christmas, the time when all the children receive their goodies. Three of us children were living at home and Mum was carrying her ninth child. We were all looking forward to seeing what Santa would bring and the best Christmas treat of all... the lovely meal that went with the presents.

The day passed quickly, night was soon upon us and the clouds were passing over a full moon. It was time to hang up our stockings before going upstairs, but before this, we kissed Mum and Dad goodnight, then the three of us went upstairs to our beds. All of us were very excited as we crawled into the small beds and tried to go to sleep.

God, it was very cold outside, even inside below the bedding. The temperature must have been well below zero. The dim light bulb in the attic revealed shadows everywhere I looked. None of us kids felt tired this night. We were hoping to see Father Christmas but not being able to keep awake, we all fell into a deep sleep. The last thing I can remember was the yapping of a female fox somewhere outside in the deep snow.

While we were asleep, our parents must have worked very hard to make us believe Santa had come. The food we had left for the reindeers had to be cleared away and all the chores had to be done before our parents went to bed, knowing that at the crack of dawn they would be awoken by us.

As our parents expected, all of us were awake early, and as the rays of the sun came through the attic window, I was slipping my trousers and shirt on and I just about beat my sisters to the top of the stairs. At the bottom of the stairs was just like fairy land, for long strings of popcorn were everywhere one looked. Then we spied the stockings; they were laden with candy and a red apple showing at the top, and looking down at the floor I could see one long line of white popcorn that led around a corner of the room. As we followed the line, a huge Christmas tree appeared and again it was draped with extra large white popcorn. The green needles of the tree were really beautiful. In between the branches nestled the presents Saint Nicholas had brought. Looking closer, my little sister pointed to where she had left the food for the reindeers. It had all gone.

Opening up the presents was exciting. I had four toy soldiers, two balloons and a very large bar of chocolate. I was elated with what I had received. My two sisters both got a well-dressed wooden doll and a couple of other items, including a bar of milky candy. We were so excited and pleased, we all rushed over to our parents to give them a kiss and cuddle and to wish them a very happy Christmas.

Our plates were piled up with goodies as we sat down at the very long table. Mum had not let us down, for this was one of the best dinners we had ever enjoyed. It was very rare for us to have a table laden with such a load of treats but it did not take long for the food to disappear. This was very typical of a Christmas in the 1930s, for money was scarce and the recession had only just reached its end.

My father worked until late at night, without a break, for six days a week with no time off. There were no paid holidays when we were brought up.

Christmas Day was the exception. So you can see what a special time it was for all the family. Both parents worked equally hard to bring up and care for the family. Christmas was the time of year when everyone could go to their local church, if there was one, and pray for a better year to come.

I was just nearing my eighth birthday and now instead of three of us living at my home, there were six. Ralph, at thirteen, was the eldest and the youngest, Edwin, was five. Every child born into the family meant another mouth to feed, and to make matters worse, Mum was pregnant again and this would be her tenth child. I heard my father talking to himself saying 'never again' and remember wondering what he meant, though when I grew up I understood.

All of us children went to the same school and, even today, I can recall the top two teachers' names, Mrs Taylor and Miss Rideout. These two were the top two, but the one I knew very well was Mrs Gould. There was a lot of bullying at the school; it just seemed as though the ones who had the least were the most vulnerable.

Two ugly brothers were always picking on me and every day they would trip me up or smack me and many days I arrived home with plenty of bruises. Then my dad noticed I had a cut behind the ear.

'Where and when did you get that?' he said and when I told him, he got upset. 'Now look here, my little peanut' – that was my nickname – 'you must stick up for yourself and give as good as you get, for if you don't, they will think you are a pushover.'

It took me a long time to figure out how a boy of eight could defeat two brothers who were a year older than him. At last an idea came to mind. If I could save them both from harm, they would become friends and thus leave me alone. I thought about this for a very long time and then, out of the blue, the problem was solved.

Washington Street was a mile from where I lived and all my family knew an elderly but gentle man, who lived in a very old white house with a long fence around his back garden. He owned a huge, ferocious dog that always chased after anyone who came near his place. I proceeded to put my plan into action. Waiting to see them come to the street corner took quite a long time but at last I spotted the two brothers. Raising my arm and clenching my fist, I shook it at them, turned around and started to run.

Sure enough they ran toward me but I slowed up just as I approached the wooden fence. They very nearly caught me as I dropped down to the dry ground on the other side. Just as they both put their hands out to grab me, bounding across the big green garden was the huge, fierce and ugly looking dog. He soon had the two boys standing against an upright post, crying with fright, and the barking dog put his paws upon one of the boys' shoulders. This was enough to make both lads sit on the ground just beneath the fence and yell with all their might for someone to save them.

I was standing by a birch tree in the garden, watching as this was happening and was fascinated at the pair of bullies' behaviour, for the huge dog was trying to reach the two and showing his teeth and really growling. They just stood there, absolutely petrified. Picking up a stick fallen at the bottom of the tree, I went towards the boys and they gazed at me coming, still with fear and disbelief in their eyes. They did not drop their hands until I threw the stick for the growling dog to chase.

The boys did not know that the dog and I had been pals for quite some time, for during the long weekends I would take him for a walk. Tiger, for that was his name, would always chase a thrown stick, so I drew back my arm and threw the stick back toward the house. Tiger turned from the boys to run after it, leaving the bullies and me to run back to the fence and drop to the other side.

The dog returned to the place of our departure to bark and growl and the two boys put their arms over my skinny shoulders and jokingly said what they would have done to the dog if he had come any closer. I took no notice of what they said, for I knew Tiger would not hurt a fly.

That evening, I told my dad what I had done. I have never seen him laugh so much before. He rested a hand on top of my head. 'Peanut, let's hope this episode will change the two Jones brothers' attitude toward you.'

As it happened, we all turned out to be good chums. They never will forget the day I saved them from a 'blood-crazy' dog. Sometimes I did feel

29

quite guilty about the way I had fooled those boys but there were other times when I was glad I had done so.

In my childhood days, we would have been considered a very poor family, but there were many others who had nothing. My brothers and sisters did not wear shoes when it was warm. We went barefooted. I think the soles of our feet were so hard, we could probably have walked on glass and not be cut. The only time shoes were needed was in the winter and then we would all wear lumbering rubbers, a kind of boot. So you see, Dad saved money in the summer but spent more in the winter months. During this time it took up most of his wages. I would like to think we were worth it but as I grew older I began to feel sorry for my parents. They gave us everything they could afford and went without themselves but when we were young, we never understood what our dad and mum sacrificed. In all my early years, the two of them never once had a holiday, apart from Christmas Day. It was just work and more work – no wonder the family always went to bed early.

The stress and strain of all the work must have made them very tired. Even when my father was not at the textile mill, he was working at his big vegetable garden, growing the food for Mum to bottle for the winter. This meant that although my father did his share of work by bringing in all the money, my poor mum had all us kids to bring up, as well as doing all the chores, including the 'laying down' of food for the cold winter months that lay ahead.

There were lots of times as a lad when I got very hungry, but I knew there was a kind old lady who worked at the bakery shop in Camden. She had a lovely face and seemed to be smiling all the time. The shop sold all types of bread and cakes. I particularly recollect the nice creamy buns and the wonderful tarts that were always on display. Every time a hungry youngster passed the window, he always stopped to look at them.

One day I was just about ready to move on, when the old woman came to the door. I thought she was going to tell me to pass on, but instead she gave me two pieces of rum cake, and, boy, it tasted delicious! From that day forth, all the poor hungry children stopped at this shop.

I wonder if the shop still exists. All of the poorest kids of Camden will remember this shop, as the owners would not let any child go away feeling hungry. All a child had to do was ask the kind little old lady for a 'bite to eat'.

When the autumn and winter months arrived, there was no such thing as having a hot bath. The house had no central heating. The only hot water available came from the iron cooking range. However, all the family once a week had a washdown bath, taking kettles of hot water from the stove and pouring it into a huge tin basin and mixing cold water with it for cleaning oneself. This was the usual procedure during the cold weather but in late spring and summer the bathing was different again.

The river was only a mile from home, so all boys, and even girls, gathered at the river cove called Shirt Tail Point. Then all of us would get undressed and jump into the water to either swim across the old river to Bass Rock or just generally throw white pebbles into the water and dive in to pick them up. This could go on all day. If there was a girl with us, no one would take any notice of her for, believe me, in those days she was just having a good time like the rest of us. The girls more often than not would be swimming with each other and they all knew they would be safe from any harm. There was sometimes a bit of flirting, but this was very rare indeed.

Behind our house there lay a large pool of water that was, in places, quite deep. I used to search for tadpoles and sometimes would catch the odd toad or bullfrog. My dad kept on about his trips on the ocean and, being a young lad, I wanted to find out how it felt to be on the water in a boat and it did not take me long to figure out where I would find something that would take the place of a boat. Resting against the wall in the lean-to where the toilet stood was the top of a large wooden trunk. Just what a youngster needed. Dragging it behind me, I got to the edge of the water with a small piece of wood as a paddle. I got on to the trunk top and pushed my home-made boat away from the side of the big wide pool. I was a very lucky boy, it floated in the water, mainly, I think because I weighed so little. All day long I played at being a sailor. I must have paddled a hundred times around this damn jagged pool of very calm water. When, at last, I got tired of the trunk-top boat, I left it to go home. My mum asked me what I had been up to and I told her a little white lie, for I knew if I told her the truth that my small bottom would surely have been smacked! When I said, 'I've only had a walk through the cemetery,' she believed me.

There was no such thing as pocket money in my childhood. So to make some money, boys would go to the river that ran beside the old textile mills, to see if we could find metals such as brass, copper or lead. Everyone searching for these metals in the river always got wet but to a poor boy this was well worth it. Then the metal was taken to the two Jewish men in Rockland. This became the procedure. The first buyer was approached and when he offered a price he would always be told 'so and so had offered more.' In order to get the old metal, the other man would offer more.

Returning old Coca Cola bottles also got me some extra pennies. It was not much but it did not cost much to see a film at the theatre. Anyway, a friend could always be found to open the door, so I could get in to see the film for free. The manager of the cinema soon put a stop to this. How? Well, it was quite easy. He took pity on me. Every so often, he let me in for free, providing I gave him my word that I would not try to gain entry again, or let anyone in myself.

It wasn't until we moved to our third home that I

sold waterlilies, gathered from a cove near the old textile watermill. I had to wade through the river to get them. I plundered the lot and charged ten cents for three water lilies. I gave the money I had earned to my mum, who was busy at the time bottling green beans to put into the cellar for the winter. She smiled as I lay two dollars on the table. I was really pleased to be able to help the family.

During my early teens, in my school holiday I thought of another way to make money. I knew there were many small cabins around the great lake where the owners came up once a year for their holiday. I also knew they wanted bait for their fishing. I put a large board beside the road, nailed to a post and in large letters wrote 'FROGS FOR SALE'.

After collecting the inch-long green and brown frogs and making sure they were secure, I was ready to make a sale. My best customer was a Doctor Codman, from the state of Massachusetts. He was very kind to me and he got very friendly with my father. Unfortunately, everything has its season, for the Doctor put five dollars in my hand one day and said to me smiling, 'Good luck, my friend Buddy. We will meet again and the money I give you is for a haircut,' and he waved as he left.

Teenage Years

My sister Freda had asked our parents if Thelma and I would like to have a holiday with her and her husband Gwen at Cape Rosia. That weekend, we packed and got into the 'rumble seat' – the rear part of the car that the two of us could sit in. It had a half-moon-shaped door that shut over the top of us, to keep the weather out. Mum sat in the front beside Dad. He drove many miles until we reached a large town called Bucksport.

Passing over the bridge to the other side of the harbour took but a few minutes. I believe the toll was fifty cents, a lot of money in those days. The town of Bucksport had history going back a very long time. It was probably built around the eighteenth century.

Whilst passing through it, my father stopped at an ancient-looking graveyard. He and Mum seemed to know this place very well, for they led me to a grave. 'Look at this, Peanut. There is a legend about this grave. It is the reason why a man was put to death for a wicked murder and why the state abolished capital punishment. Many years ago, he was hanged and up to the time they hanged him, he always pleaded his innocence. Before they hanged him he cursed the crowd of onlookers saying, 'To prove you are hanging an innocent man you will find the black picture of a leg on my grave stone.' And sure enough, there it was. After stopping here for a short time we were on our way again. I was pleased my dad had stopped for the grave stone, as the legend was very interesting.

We drove up one country lane after another and at last saw our sister Freda with her husband Gwen, standing just outside the doorway of a lovely little wooden house. We kids jumped up in the rumble seat to shout, 'Here we are, sis.' She gave the two of us a kiss and took us into the house.

After having a bite to eat, Mum and Dad got into the car and as the car was pulling away, Dad leaned out of the window to wave to us, then the car disappeared from view. The rest of the day went very quickly and, as the dusk settled in, it became quite dark outside. We were then shown to our bedroom. This would have been the first time that my sister and I had been away from our parents for any length of time.

The next day came and we started to miss them but a snowstorm came during the night and this took our minds off our parents, as now the two of us could have fun playing in the snow. In the afternoon, Thelma was helping her sister cook dinner. In the meantime, Gwen took his shotgun and the two of us went rabbit hunting.

Gwen was no different from my own clan, for like my own brother Ralph – he did not kill because he liked to – it was to provide food during the winter months.

I learned a great deal about hunting rabbits with my brother-in-law. I already knew they turned from grey to white in the wintertime but I never could understand why the rabbits stood up on their hind legs to listen whenever someone whistled, for they became an easy target for the hunter. The day ended with me learning even more about nature and on the way back to my two sisters I was also told how to tell the difference between an edible wild mushroom and the poisonous ones.

Freda's house had a dirt road just in front of it and a small garden at the rear. All around it was a mixture of many types of trees and bushes but looking through and over these could be seen the mighty Atlantic Ocean, with waves smashing into grey-brown rocks. After seeing this raw part of nature, I began strolling further down the dirty road. My brother-in-law had told me about the little old house about a mile away. This was where Ralph's in-laws lived. Coming around a huge bend, I saw the shape of a desolate house. All the snow the night before had disappeared and the sunlight glistened off the water pail hanging just above the water well in front of the overgrown garden. I slowly walked to the fence and began shouting, 'Hello, is anybody at home?'

A little woman appeared from nowhere. 'What

do you want, young man?' she asked, and as she spoke, she was eyeing me up and down.

'I'm your daughter's brother-in-law,' I told her. 'My sister and I are staying with Freda and Gwen just up the road.'

Then the lady pointed a finger at me to stand aside, walking to the door as she did so. 'Well please, young man, do not gander about. Come on in, for I'm about to start an operation on a very sick rooster.'

Putting her hand on my shoulder, she led me into a room that really needed a good clean. There, on a table, lay the rooster. He never moved until the old lady slowly approached him. I sat on the floor, fascinated at what she was about to do. She had taken the rooster from the table and put its head beneath the bird's wing. It immediately became as still as death and didn't move an inch.

'Now, my young lad, watch what I am about to do,' she said, plucking feathers from the rooster's breast.

She held up a sharp knife and then proceeded to open the bird's chest. Then, putting her fingers inside the chest, she very gently took out its fat crop and was holding it in her hands to slit it apart. The food, plus a nail the rooster had eaten, fell out of the crop.

'This is why we had such a very sick bird,' she said, as she pointed at the nail. Believe it or not, she sewed the crop together with a needle and a bit of thread, also doing the bird's open breast at the same time. I closed my eyes with disbelief as she put the rooster on the floor. With that, the bird ran out of the open door, crowing as he ran back to the hens. In all my years I'd never seen anything like that. As I bade the old woman goodbye, to make my way to my sister's house, I was still trying to work out how she had cured that rooster.

My sister and I were about five days into our holiday. Everything was looking fine. Thelma was visiting the old home where I had seen the frail lady operate on the rooster. However, later that day, my sister returned sobbing and looked very distressed.

She would not tell me the reason why, but my older sister took her by the hand and the two of them went into the bedroom for a chat. They stayed in the room for quite a while and when the two of them finally came out Freda and her husband went outside the house and conversed very softly. Quite a long time later, Freda's husband took us aside to tell us our few days with them had come to an end. He made the excuse that he and Freda had to meet another couple very soon for a very important reason, so he had no choice but to send the pair of us home. As a youngster I knew he was making an excuse and even today I still have never found out the reason, but it seems obvious now that the poor old dear had died.

Now, how were we to make the journey back to Camden? We were to go by boat and I smiled when I heard the owner's name, Goofy. I know for a fact that if my elder sister had known the danger we would go through, the trip would have been cancelled. The long journey involved going across a stretch of water four miles wide and after that, another ten miles sailing around five or six small islands. This trip could be done quite easily but looking up at the sky, even at my age, I felt a bit scared. The sail boat was about eighteen feet long and there was no cabin, just a bench at the stern. Being only about thirteen years old, I did as I was told and certainly never knew what lay ahead. As there was no more room in the stern to sit, I sat down near the front, just under the upright mast pole.

Thelma and Goofy sat at the back. He was steering the boat with the outboard motor. Thelma had a brown rabbit and she was holding it in her lap and talking to it. So we set out on our long journey. It was early in the morning. In two hours the boat made very good progress. Then the winds started to blow and the boat plunged deeper into the swell of the waves. I still was not worried, but looking at Goofy's face made me wonder why I shouldn't be, for all of his features looked as white as a sheet and, to me, he even seemed to be praying.

The front of the boat went up and then dipped below the waves. No one could see the land in the distance. As if we didn't have enough trouble, the damn outboard motor packed up, leaving us to the mercy of the dark icy sea. As the sound of the motor became silent, Thelma was crying, and the poor animal she was holding was trying to get out of her arms. The yard arm was swinging recklessly about. Goofy shouted to me, 'See if you can free that sail, Buddy. We cannot go much further like this.' Above the sound of the wind I again heard him yell, 'Do it quickly – this is our last chance!'

Can anyone imagine a boy of my age doing what was asked of him? But I had to try. Kneeling down, I grabbed the tall mast to pull myself up, the boat dipping and rolling every which way. I then reached for the oar. God, I really was frightened and could not stand this for much longer. I was lucky for, although I knew very little about this type of boat, I did see why the sail would not go up the mast. A small ring prevented the canvas from sliding up the pole. Placing the oar under the ring, I pushed upward as the craft's front went down. Good job I had my arm around the mast, for as the ring was dislodged, the canvas shot up the pole. I must admit, it was a good thing Goofy was sitting at the rudder, for no way could I have returned to the stern. Anyway, before I could have reached the stern, the boat certainly would have turned over, drowning the lot of us. However, the sail boat took off like a bat out of hell and within fifteen minutes we were near the coastline.

With a look of relief on his face, Goofy navigated the boat into the harbour that lay very close to the bridge of Bucksport. The wharf where we were to dock had a crowd of people standing about, watching our every move.

'Are you mad or just plain stupid?' one of the onlookers shouted, as he looked at Goofy. 'To make the crossing on a day like this and putting these children's lives at risk, you must be off your head.' No one took much notice of what he said but there was a lot of muttering in the crowd.

Many times later I thought of what the man had said. And he was right, for we started our trip across the channel in the morning and it was late evening when we got across that expanse of water. All of us got out of the boat at that time feeling tired and lucky to be alive. We had to rest and continue our journey to Camden early in the morning. Before doing this, my sister gave the rabbit to a little girl she saw close by and we refuelled the boat with petrol.

The giant sun was well over the horizon as we all climbed back into the boat. As we made ourselves comfortable, the boat was pushed away from the wharf, leaving the crowd of people behind. The outboard motor pushed the boat about a mile. Halfway around a small island, we motored into a big cove and pulled the boat up on a rock-strewn beach to rest for the night. None of us had a good night's sleep despite being dog tired. I think the stress that we had experienced the day before had taken its toll. The ground was hard to lie on and boy was it cold. All night long the sound of singing kept me awake.

When morning finally arrived, I found the singing was coming from a tight length of thin island grass, blowing back and forth in the sea breeze and making a humming sound. The large bright sun was well into the sky as we got into the boat again and we must have gone a few miles before passing another piece of land. Goofy informed us that there was only one more island and then we would be home. My sister pointed to the leeward side of the boat and there following us were five dolphins, going up and down in the calm waters, but always a few yards away.

After a while, seagulls were flying all around us and sure enough in the distance Negro Island came into view. To the right of the large island came the majestic beauty of Mount Betty. Everyone on the sail boat put their hands above their heads for there was a time earlier when not one of us thought we would reach our destination. The sight of Camden harbour was before us and, as the sail was put down, I used the oar to glide the boat to the wharf. All of us got off the craft, looked at each other and not a word was spoken. We three had come through a harsh nightmare on that long journey. Mum and Dad were really surprised to see us, for they had thought Freda was to keep us for at least another two weeks. My parents were also upset at the way she had sent the two of us packing, not realising how dangerous the sea could be, especially at that time of the year.

While Thelma and I had been on holiday, lots of unexpected incidents were about to happen. The family were about to move to the third house. Although I had overheard my parents talking of moving, I had no idea it was already built and located in such beautiful scenery.

It just took one's breath away! I marvelled at how my father and brothers had built the place and the time it took was hard to believe. All of us were certainly amazed and for a while we just gazed at it.

The weekend for moving arrived and all of us packed our belongings and carried them to the old Ford truck. We all took our time, as there were a few tears shed, at least by the four children who had been born in the old wooden hand-made building on Sand Street.

Memories galore that were left would never be forgotten. But no one can live in the past, for time always moves on. My mother and all us children were soon dropped off at our new home and we jokingly called it Nelsonville. Four other families lived just across the road from us.

Dad and my two elder brothers returned to collect the heavier items, such as the table, chairs and the large black cooking range.

The large house was built on top of a rocky rise, with the main road just in front of it. Across the road and not far away, the wide river flowed, passing four dams before arriving at the sea in the Camden harbour. The giant height of Mount Betty towered in the distance, showing all the beautiful green-needled pine trees stretching along one mountain to another that was even higher, called Mount Megunticook, where a large white cross was visible. This was put there in the eighteenth century, in memory of a young lady who died falling off the cliff.

We took a while to settle in and it was at this time that I thought of making money from selling waterlilies, the brown and green frogs, and, of course, there was always the metal to sell for scrap.

The winter of 1935 was one of the coldest I had experienced and the snow was so deep one had to climb out of the attic window to shovel it away from the door. We made skis out of wooden barrow staves (flat pieces of wood) to walk in the snow. This was also the year I was chased up a tree by a brown bear. Why he was not hibernating I will never know. It was near spring time and so maybe he awoke feeling hungry and I was to be his next meal!

There was not much difference between our house in Sand Street and the one we now lived in. It was larger and all the children slept in separate beds in the large attic. The outdoor toilet was still in use but the water well was quite a long distance up the dirt road and, if anything, the well water did taste fresher, but as I bent to look into the hole I was surprised to see three rainbow trout swimming in it. I was later told by my dad that these fish kept the water 'insect free'. It was very pure water and to drink it was like drinking water from the gods. But to get it, one had to walk way down a long, winding dirt path and the pails had to be full. At the time, this meant quite a few trips were needed, for everyone was always thirsty and it was nice to know water was always available.

At fourteen, I still liked to play games, and some were very dangerous. Our best game was 'red shirt'. Someone in our group would wear a red shirt and have a fifteen-minute head start, then the rest of us would have to find him. The boy who caught him would have the privilege of wearing the red shirt and the game would continue. On this occasion, I was the one wearing the shirt and I headed for the woods. I knew beyond a shadow of a doubt that the rest would not catch me. Pushing aside small bushes and passing around tall maple trees, I headed towards my destination. Then, I thought, why not have some fun? Leave a trail for the others to follow and see what they do.

Fifteen minutes passed and I knew they were somewhere behind me. I slowed up as I approached the river to let the hunters catch sight of me, knowing that it would be just a quick glance. I then spied what I was looking for. In front of me was the tall tree that had a thick rope stretching from its trunk, across the fast-running river, to another tree on the other side.

Now, I know it was madness to do what I did, but young boys do ridiculous things. Climbing up to the rope, I lay outstretched on it and started to pull my way across. Luckily, I got three quarters of the way over before the mishap occurred. My body slipped off, leaving me still holding the rope but hanging above the rushing water below me. I knew to reach the other side I would have to use my legs to pull myself the rest of the way. I really did not think I could reach the other side, but I did and climbing down was easy.

I fell in a heap at the bottom of the giant oak tree. Having a rest, I then looked across the river and saw my friends chatting together. I could not hear what they were saying but could see their lips moving, but the distance was too great to hear anything. I had a pretty good idea though, as one of them pointed at the rope. Everyone on the other side was shaking their heads from side to side. But there was one more daring than the others.

He was seen pointing at the oak tree with the rope and walking towards it as he did so. No, you damn fool, I thought to myself. Surely there could not be another fool like me? I was wrong, though, for he was about to do as I had done. If I had only known what was about to happen I would have given him the damn red shirt, but it was too late. I really am sure all of the friends with him did their level best to stop him from going.

One of the big boys in the group grabbed his arm but he just brushed him aside. Reaching the giant tree, he started the short climb up the rope. I watched him as he was doing exactly the same thing I had done. I really thought he would make it over but I was to be proven wrong since, just yards away from his goal, he lost his balance, tried to grab the rope, missed and shouted as he plummeted into the boulder-strewn rushing water below. Instantly, there were shouts of 'Oh no!' and everyone rushed to the river bank but he could not be seen. Where I lay, I could see things the others could not and as he hit the water the strong current carried his body quickly down the river.

Leaping from my place of concealment, I shouted across the river, 'Go quickly down the river, past the rocks, just keep your eyes open!' On both sides of the wide river, all of us followed the river bank. Coming to a sharp bend, we both saw each other at the same time. Moses, his nickname, had somehow pulled himself from the river and was just sitting on an old tree stump.

'You damn fool!' I said 'there was no need to do such a stupid thing. Why did you do it?'

'I wanted the red shirt,' he replied.

'Well, take the damn thing and I hope it fits you.'

Taking it off took but a few seconds and as the others waded across the water he put the dry shirt on to his wet body.

The doom and gloom left every face and we all went home. Moses was not seriously hurt – he only had a few bruises. But after this ordeal we never played red shirt again. That year, the river had many casualties and I know that during my childhood there were at least four deaths from drowning. So my friends and I knew Moses could easily have been the fifth.

A boy in his teens had plenty of leisure time, for by law, he was not allowed to work full time. He was just allowed to do a paper round, but only living in a small village, few were hired. The population of Camden exceeded two thousand houses and was spread over a distance of ten miles. It was too far for any one person to deliver papers, especially youngsters, and so anyone who wanted a daily paper went to the corner shop. Children had to go to school until they were eighteen, and then they had the choice to go to college or find a full-time job. Anyway, as I was only about fifteen at the time, I still had a few years to go.

The plight of my friend Moses brings back a memory I must describe. A wide river started its long journey from a dam at the huge lake of Megunticook. This resulted in parts of the river being rapids and in some places huge coves were made. The water flowed past Nelsonville and about two miles of flowing water was held back by another dam. In fact, there were another three dams before it went into the harbour of Camden. The reason why I'm describing this river is the near disaster that occurred during a very cold winter.

In sub-zero weather, the water would freeze and leave all of the coves with ice that was two feet thick. Owing to the force of the water, there were certain parts that did not freeze over. This was to be mainly in the middle, a section spanning about sixty or seventy feet. My brothers John, Ralph and myself went ice skating on a very large cove of the river and boy we were having a great time. My two brothers could skate like professionals. As for me, I hadn't a clue but was still having fun. Both of my brothers were told to keep an eye on me but were so engaged in what they were doing they forgot. I went very close to the cold running water, when a large chunk of ice broke away from where I was standing, leaving me floating on a raft of ice. As the raft picked up speed, I had one hell of a job standing on it. My brothers had dropped what they were doing and were trying to keep up with me as they chased the raft along the snow-covered river bank. They were yelling at me to hang on. I sure as hell did, for I was more frightened than they were, especially when the ice raft rounded a bend and I saw yet another dam in the distance.

About 500 yards from the dam, the current seemed to push the ice toward the bank and wasn't I a lucky lad, for I went under the overhanging branch of a very large snow-covered tree. I was doubly lucky for, as I leapt up, I was able to grab the branch just as the piece of ice tipped up to go over the dam. Pulling my way to safety was a bit difficult but at long last I rested below the tree. My brothers were on the scene almost immediately, and the relief showed in their faces. Shedding a tear or two, the three of us left that place of near-tragedy and I remember both my brothers telling me 'don't tell Dad' and I certainly never did.

It would be very hard to pick the season I liked the most, for there were always different things to do in each one. The one I would choose as being the worst would be the very beginning of the cold winter months. To begin with, there seemed to be less food about, so many a meal was lost, and then there was the walk to school of at least four to five miles. It was very rare for the school bus to turn up. This was mostly due to the huge amount of snow on the roads. It then became a case of walking, and more often than not we would be late.

If you did get there on time, half the pupils wouldn't have. For school dinner, a youngster was lucky if they had a sandwich made with their mum's home-baked bread. The walk home from school was always against the cold north winds blowing through our clothes and, once arriving home, even the coldest room felt warm. But there were some good times, like building igloos, ice-fishing, sleighing and making snowmen.

My brother Ralph took me grey-squirrel hunting. Believe it or not, they provided quite a tasty meal, all meat and no fat. All day long we walked, not always looking for squirrels, but just taking in the lovely scenery and talking about this or that. I was about three yards behind and, just as I took another step, he raised his shotgun and fired. A dead partridge lay close by. He handed me the gun as he stooped to pick it up, and then he gave me the bird. I put it under my arm and carried on walking.

Ralph reached into his red padded coat and produced a-slingshot. He said, 'Squirrels would have too much lead in them to eat, so we must use this old-fashioned gadget.'

We must have walked four or five miles when he spotted the animal sitting on a branch. Without hesitation, he left me and slowly went toward the giant oak tree. A few yards from it, he drew back the rubber band and fired a ball bearing.

The poor animal fell from its perch, to land just in front of us, and as I was carrying the partridge, he put the squirrel inside his shirt and buttoned it up. I don't think we had gone more than fifty yards when he let out a terrible scream. The animal he had put inside his shirt wasn't dead – it had only been stunned by the ball bearing. My brother was going mad as he ripped open his shirt. The animal had taken bite after bite to get free, leaving blood all over his naked chest. The squirrel jumped out and quickly ran off, leaving my poor brother in terrible pain. This ended our day of hunting.

Poor Ralph was in pain for at least two to three weeks. You can bet we never forgot that day and the only thing we achieved was having partridge for dinner.

PART TWO:
Man at War

Conscription

Two days after my nineteenth birthday I got my papers for conscription into the army. I was drafted on 29 January 1943. I was only a young man, but was soon to learn that this would be the second phase of my life.

I was in my third year at the high school when I heard over the radio that Pearl Harbor had been bombed by the Japanese. This, above all, was bad tidings for as soon as the news was heard, President Roosevelt declared war, not only against the Japanese but also on Germany, making America legally at war with both countries.

John Jr, my brother, was already in the army when I received my call-up papers. Soon the day arrived when I was to call at the interview room at Portland, Maine. This was to meet a panel of doctors to pass my medical.

I passed the test with no problems and I remember one of the doctors asking me if I wanted to join the forces to which I replied, 'I have an aching trigger finger.'

I now realise at my age that one makes mistakes and I was young and foolish, but no one can turn the clock back.

I was to report to a camp at Fort Devon, Massachusetts. This was just after my birthday but I did have about three days with my family before I reported. My mum and sisters were very tearful, for this was the first time in my life that I had travelled alone. Arriving at the camp, we all lined up and each man was given the full kit, which included the shoes and trousers, even down to the ammunition belt, canteen and rifle with bayonet. With all this gear I felt just like the well-offs!

We were all taken to a train station and were on our way to Little Rock, Arkansas, to commence our six weeks of basic training.

It did not start off too well for me. I was not used to taking orders and told the corporal in charge to 'eff off' and he put me on a charge. They made me walk from five o'clock in the afternoon until ten o'clock that night, with a full field pack and rifle, walking back and forth until I said how sorry I was to the corporal in charge.

Then after three weeks I came down with pneumonia, so I had to wait not six weeks but nine before I could even be passed out to join a regiment. This meant, of course, that the first lot I did my training with had already left and I had to leave with the second group. Before ending my nine weeks, we went on parade marching down a long street and through a town. This was a wonderful occasion for me, for I felt so proud to have been taught so many things about army life, such as how to take an M1 rifle apart in the dark and to reassemble it. Then it was the rifle range and the use of hand grenades. The most important thing was the art of hand-to-hand combat and survival. It's surprising what one remembers of one's life and the unexpected things that can happen and usually did. I still to this day say Franklin D Roosevelt was the very best president. I wrote a letter to him when I was at school and even received a reply. I had this letter in my possession for many years but unfortunately, somewhere in my hectic life, I misplaced it. Maybe someday it will turn up. But something better than this did turn up.

After our march through Little Rock we were all told to fall out and a few of us were lounging about and doing nothing when three men approached us.

The man in the middle looked familiar. He stopped just in front of me and said, 'Keep up the good work, soldier, and may God protect you.'

A few more supportive words were spoken, which I cannot recall, and then he shook my hand and as he departed the soldier close by came hurrying up, 'Do you know who that was?' and I shook my head. 'For your information, he is the commander-in-chief, the President himself.'

At that time, I felt over the moon for I had really met and exchanged words with him.

The following week I finished basic training and all the men who passed this went to the railway station and boarded the train. Quite a while later the train pulled into the state of Tennessee and lorries were waiting for us as we disembarked. Then every soldier was taken to

Camp Forest to become part of Company A315 Infantry Regiment, where we were to resume training of a different kind. This was to make us into a fully trained combat infantry unit. Again, we were inoculated but for a few of the men this meant horror, for I had already seen many young soldiers of eighteen to twenty, faint at the sight of a needle. They could stand up to facing a man with a gun but never a needle, which I could not understand.

From day one, in this new situation, I got on well with the officers and sergeants, plus all the other new soldiers. Maybe it was because I had learnt a lot from my lessons in basic training. In this camp we were to learn more than basics. Apart from the inspections, there was marching, the rifle range and hand grenade practice. When we were not performing sentry guard duties, or even being kitchen police, then it was always roll call and unarmed combat.

All of this went on for at least two months and then on the grapevine we heard we would, very shortly, be sent on manoeuvres.

A week later the high command informed us we would be bound for Arizona in two days time. Now, from Camp Forest to Arizona was hundreds of miles. We travelled by train for nearly two days and then by lorries, to be dropped off hours later on the outskirts of a very huge arid desert called Death Valley. Then the whole regiment was billeted in rows of large canvas tents. Everything was so different from the scenery we had left. Sand and more sand and cacti as far as the eye could see. The sun was so hot that an egg could be fried on a flat rock. Believe me, it took days for me to feel at home in this wide expanse of heat and sand. Temperatures rose to one hundred and twenty degrees Fahrenheit outside. In the courtyard stood tripods and large canvas bags hung down between them and over each bag was a round wooden cover. It was filled with water. The water, when drank, was as cold as ice. No one could figure out why this was, but it really tasted great! We were also issued with saltpetre for dehydration, to take with the water.

There had been no snakes or other such perils in the other camps I had been in. But here it was different. It was not unknown for a sidewinder (a small rattlesnake) to be found inside a tent, so one had to be careful at all times, because not only were there snakes, but also gila monsters (a type of poisonous lizard) and tarantulas. To be perfectly safe, before shoes were put on, they had to be turned upside down and shaken because scorpions sometimes crept into them during the night.

One thing I must stress in that, although the living conditions were nothing to write home about, the scenery was out of this world, for not only was it beautiful during the daylight hours but the yellow moon cast shadows of the cacti when it shone during the nights. In fact, the moon looked so large in the sky that I truly felt I could reach out and touch it.

They told me this was because of the lack of air

in the desert. It rains only about once a year in the desert of Death Valley and I was lucky enough to be there at the right time. Words cannot describe the beauty I observed. To see so many flowers of different colours on these giant cacti with their sweet perfume filling the air. Whenever this occurred it was always called 'the painted desert' and believe me it was. All of this lasted for about an hour. Then the rain clouds passed overhead and the sun beamed down and within minutes the flowers had died and vanished, to become a desert of sand once again.

Before and during our training we had some very long breaks and so this meant that groups of us could go and see different places.

I swam in a river cove that flowed in the great Grand Canyon of Colorado, not the white rapid water that gushed further on down but in the calmer waters. At least I can say that I swam in it. Then I visited New Mexico and even went to Mexico in South America. I had to go through the border and was astonished at the amount of pure silver objects for sale and should have bought a few, for today they would be worth a small fortune. Staying in Mexico overnight was a mistake, because my chum and I could not find a place to kip for the night but eventually ended up sleeping just above a roller-skating rink. It turned out to be a very sleepless night, for the noise kept us awake all night. Then, a week later, a lot of the soldiers went to a large arena to see a few movie stars. The Bob Hope concert was quite an event.

This may sound like a grand holiday to some, but try walking twenty miles with a full field pack on your back and carrying a rifle in heat of at least one hundred and twenty degrees. Then, for a bit of good measure, almost falling over a long diamond-back rattlesnake that turned up from out of nowhere. This episode in the manoeuvres was an endurance test to find out how much a soldier could take before he gave in and had to sit down beside the line of marching men. We were allowed a ten-minute break every ten miles walked. The first ten miles were not too bad, although we were very glad of the break at the end of them. But after that, each mile was a strain on every muscle in the body.

As time passed, one man would fall by the wayside, then another. The exhausting heat and the tiredness were telling on the soldiers. I remember quite well just tramping along and, for a laugh, starting to whistle and to sing 'give me my boots and saddle'. Just by doing this everyone seemed to cheer up and all down the line everyone started to laugh and joined in singing the song. At long last we reached the halfway mark, turned around and started on the return, heading back to our canvas pup tents. These were a small backpacked one-man tent, to save time by not having to 'dig in'.

The return was as bad as the outward journey.

The only difference being that the men who had dropped out had been picked up and taken back to base camp. This left the soldiers on the long return thinking maybe we were the dopes in not doing the same. The second day passed and the men who made the trip (all twenty miles), were upgraded to first-class privates and to my utter surprise I was also made into the number-one scout.

Maybe, in a way, I was paid for helping a fellow soldier friend, by carrying his rifle and equipment, which helped him to finish the long walk. I also remember carrying a very small pack of razor blades. These were very useful if one was bitten by a rattlesnake. The blade could cut across the fang marks, deep enough for it to bleed. In some cases a man had to put his lips over the cut, suck out the vile poison and then spit it out. This was supposed to get rid of the poison more quickly. I'm glad to say that I was a very lucky man in not having to use the blade for this purpose, only for shaving my whiskers. I must admit though, there were times when I could have been bitten, because when I dug a hole to crawl into before it got dark I always had to be on the alert for orders from the captain and this could happen any time during the night.

One such incident occurred on a moonlit night. The whole company was sitting or having a nap in their foxholes, but I, being a scout, was on duty. I was informed by the officer in command, 'I want you to find your way to every dugout and inform every man that the action will begin at sun up tomorrow, six o'clock sharp!'

I never gave it a second thought at the time but that evening the moon was really bright. It cast long shadows everywhere one looked and no one would be able to see the snakes.

As I got out of my hole to inform the men of what was to happen the following morning, I could hear the snakes rattling but sure as hell I could not tell where the noise was coming from. I was lucky, as I was able to find and relay the captain's message to all of them and not be bitten. Or so I had thought, for later that day when I removed my leggings there was a mark of a snake's fangs just grazing my leg but not enough to penetrate the skin and looking at the graze marks on my left leg, I thanked Him above.

The regiment was on manoeuvres for somewhere close to three months. I will always remember the Grand Canyon, for the mountains were all the colours of the rainbow and everything from the grey of the big mighty cliffs of rock, to the green of the trees blending here and there. Then there was the river flowing between and below the upright boulders. This river had to be traversed with caution for it was known to be very dangerous. Then, inland from this river, the desert came into sight and the temperature was always very high. This was where I saw something I could never quite understand. Walking near a giant cactus and admiring the way the needles of the cactus plant grew, I tripped and fell over an object and, upon picking myself up, I looked and saw a turtle that was plodding about in the desert sands!

Whatever a person does in life it always comes to an end and not long after the twenty mile march the manoeuvres came to a halt. I'll bet not a man in the division felt sorry. The trials of hardship had ended but we were surprised how quickly everything was packed up and it was no time at all before we were ready to get on to the convoy of lorries and we all waved goodbye and left Arizona behind.

Again, it was a long ride to our destination, even though no one knew where we were bound. We were on the Pullman train for two whole days and during the early morning hours the large train arrived. We were 'drugged' with sleep as we got off the train and taken to the many army lorries that were waiting outside the station. Not long after this, probably one hour's ride, we disembarked outside a line of barracks and each platoon was designated one of the large tin-roofed buildings. It was some time before the entire regiment had taken control of the camp. Later on, we were told the camp was situated just outside Salina, Kansas, plum in the middle of the USA.

Then, at last, the big day came, for all of us had two weeks' leave to see our families before going overseas. I was lucky enough to enjoy a further break a bit later. There is not much I can relate about my short stay at home, only that if my dad had not taken out a loan for me to pay my train fare then I could not have afforded the trip. As usual, Mum, Dad and the family treated me like a long-lost son; they were lovely. As for the other people, barring a few close friends, I kept mostly to myself and had a wonderful rest. When the time came to leave my family, I had a good cry. I can just picture them now sobbing as the bus drove away from home.

When the train arrived at Portland, Maine, I got off and stopped overnight, breaking my train journey to visit my sister Freda, staying with her all day and talking about the good times, until we finally went to bed. The next morning I kissed my sister goodbye and, as I was walking to the station, I was stopped by a tramp. He asked me for ten cents to buy a cup of tea and believe it or not, that was just the amount I had in my pocket. I reluctantly handed him my last penny and I have always found in my life that it's the poor that will give to the poor, not the rich. I reached my twentieth birthday before at last arriving back at camp to mingle with my soldier friends. It was back to the roll calls, sentry duty, lights out, and rifle inspections and rifle range practice.

One day on a weekend and with nothing to do, I went for a long walk and very soon approached a tree-lined river. I was humming a tune, not taking much notice of where I was going. I noticed a robin flying from one branch to another and then I heard a young voice crying, 'Help!' Everything else was forgotten as I raced past the trees. Before me, I saw a boy just going under and, without a thought for my own safety, I raced to the water and jumped in, fully clothed. The river was so deep that I could not touch the bottom and so I swam out and was just in time to grab him as he came to the surface. He struggled a bit but I was able to take him to the river bank, where he coughed up some water and then seemed to breathe properly. The little girl who was yelling on the river side told me where the youngster lived and I was able to lead him by his hand to the house. I met his parents and they were really nice people. They both wept with joy and gratitude as I told them what had happened and they took their son into their arms for a cuddle, kissed him, crying as they did so and to my surprise smacked his bottom and sent him to bed telling him, 'How many times have we told you to stay away from the river?'

When I got back to camp, the order came officially... we were bound for overseas and this was to happen very soon. Seventy-five per cent of the men would be able to go for just a short embarkation leave before this happened, maybe for the last time. I often wondered why the army gave us another few days' holiday so quickly after the last one but they probably knew this would be the last one for many of the soldiers.

At last we were prepared and ready to face the enemy, whomever they may be. Most of us then left Kansas again to go home for two weeks and, as before, I had no money. My dad lent me the fare once again and gladly did so. Off I went by train to Camden, Maine and, realising this may be the last time I would ever see my family again, I felt quite depressed but tried not to show it. I was welcomed with open arms and lots of wet tears but I was home again and enjoyed all the lovely attention I received. John, my brother, was still away in the army and my brother, Ralph, had married just before I went into the services and had a couple of kids. My mum and dad were still plodding along but still had no money. Dad was still working from early dawn to dusk and was bringing up my two sisters and brother. Looking back on my life, we were taught to believe that maybe one day we could also be well off! As I got older, I realised that money just follows money and that is why my father never reached the top of the ladder.

This may come as a shock to some people but I can honestly say that, although I was in the forces and at war with Japan and Germany, I still did not know who Hitler or the emperor of Japan were and often wondered why I was going to war. Now, up to a point, I can understand how that might have been, for in those days we only had a battery radio and television was unheard of. The newspapers were not as popular as they are today. Therefore, we never knew what was really going on and did not know how wicked these men were. Maybe our war was with Japan, who had bombed Pearl Harbor, not with the man called Adolph Hitler from Germany.

Anyway, I must say this was one of the best leaves I had experienced from the forces and I was able to climb up Mount Betty, again to see all the beautiful scenery. The town of Camden was spread out like a huge coloured picture below and everything could be seen, even my old childhood schoolhouse. There was one thing I will remember about this odd leave... it was when my young sister Betty put her arms around me saying 'Take care of yourself, for we love you very much.' Then she stood back saying, 'God willing, we will see each other again.' Little did I know this would be her last words spoken to me, for she died at the young age of thirty-eight, whilst I was fighting abroad.

My father was a hard man who would bottle up his feelings. But as my leave was coming to an end, the two of us had a long walk up along Mountain Street. We stopped to gaze at some of the gravestones in the cemetery. He put his arm on my broad shoulder. 'Peanut,' he said, 'the world is just a very sick place so please take extra care of yourself and may the good Lord look after you, and bring you back to us.'

I believe this was the only time I had heard my father talk with such feeling and even as a young man it brought tears to my eyes and I had to look the other way.

One thing I had to do before I returned to my unit was to revisit my old school, for I had spent many a happy hour there just learning my ABCs, and wanted to meet the teachers whom I had lots of lessons with. There was also a poem I had remembered:

> In Flanders fields the poppies grow,
> Between the crosses, row on row,
> That mark our place; and in the sky
> The lark, still bravely singing, fly
> Scarce heard amid the guns below.

I cannot say why I recite this poem, maybe I had a feeling I would see the poppies. My visit to the school went fairly well. I met one or two of the teachers I knew, but the ones I most wanted to see had died, so again I left there with sadness in my heart.

Then, of course, came the day of my departure that I was dreading. I was on edge, right up to the time I had to leave. Both Mum and Dad and friends were all there at the Greyhound bus stop and, as the huge bus stopped, both parents held me and all the crowd shouted their goodbyes. They were still waving as the bus went out of sight. It was late afternoon as I arrived back at my unit to meet with nothing but doom and gloom. All around the camp was the feeling of something terrible about to happen, but this was to change. I believe it was the unexpected that made the foot soldiers unhappy and when the orders for early embarkation came everyone cheered up and were ready and eager to get on with it. Even as we got ready to travel, not one of us fully appreciated the reality of our situation.

Late in the May of 1944, we boarded a train that took us to the docks of New York. The army did not waste time and within one hour all the young soldiers from every platoon were standing to attention beside a very large liner and I could just faintly make out the name of *Queen Elizabeth*, then squad after squad went aboard the giant liner. As usual, the top brass travelled on the first-class deck and as one went down in rank, he found his sleeping bunk well below the waterline. There were hundreds of men making this long crossing. Everywhere one looked there were soldiers, double bunks and toilets. There also was an area they called the 'mess hall' where we all lined up to have our meals. Though I say 'we', that's not strictly true, for there was many a man who never ate a meal because they were seasick!

In the latter part of May the troop ship reached the port of Liverpool. We saw the docks as the liner was pulled to it by tug boats. One by one, with all his equipment, each soldier walked off the ship and, as before, a long line of lorries were waiting close at hand. The driver of each lorry went very slowly, for he would not be used to driving on the left. On and on we went to an unknown destination. Then, at last, we arrived at a huge field, covered as far as the eye could see with canvas tents. Some were large but they were mostly average-sized, with each one holding at least six men. We found out after a long rest that this camp was near the town of Macclesfield, a town near Wilmslow and Alderly Edge. At that moment, we were so tired we would have settled anywhere, even in a cemetery. We were dead beat.

Two days later, we were getting quite used to our

tent living quarters but it was still very difficult to move around. The toilet was outside and it was just a deep hole dug in the ground, with a canvas top and four sides. This certainly did not make it a four-star hotel. We did not know what was to happen next, so it made everyone feel unsettled and ill at ease. Command saw this and made up its mind to take our platoon to a place called Manchester, where we were to march through a certain part of the city and in doing this we would get to know the English people much better, but to tell the truth the accent they spoke was so strong, no one could understand what was being said, but it's very possible they could not understand our accent either. I can remember some of the comments and I do not think they were called for.

All of us young American soldiers had enough on our minds without hearing, 'Oversexed, overpaid and over here!' And, to rub it in, 'Go home, Yank!' Most of my army buddies turned a deaf ear to these, but I often thought a 'thank you' would have been nice.

I believe it came as quite a shock to hear from the division captain that on 4 June 1944, the regiment should be ready and prepared to leave early the following morning, to another unknown destination. There wasn't much sleep to be had for anybody that night, even though every soldier in the camp went to their beds very early. On the morning of 5 June, everyone was standing by to climb on to the many empty army vehicles standing in the road. The sun was just above the horizon as the large convoy of lorries started to move off. Still no one had even an idea where all of us were headed. The young soldiers were driven all day in a cramped position as space was limited but we did stop occasionally in a secluded place to relieve ourselves and have the odd 'C-ration' for our meal.

It was whilst we were having a break beside the road that something occurred that was to change the lives of many soldiers. 'Never volunteer,' was the saying in the American army, but to be quite honest no one had to, for all the soldiers were available and as luck would have it I was at the front and just about to eat a C-ration when I was taken as a volunteer.

About thirty of us were told to move aside and wait for the next line of army lorries to appear and join this group and so we waited on our own whilst the lorry we had been on went away.

An hour later, another line of transport stopped and, when they left, our group of thirty were on another one but this time I had to make friends with soldiers I never knew.

Then we moved on again and to tell the truth I was so tired I didn't care. It turned out that this was the 29th and not the 315th division.

The lorries were canvas-topped, so only the very few sitting in front and just behind the truck driver were able to see anything. I was sitting at the rear and so was able to see a few of the country folk as the vehicle went by. The weather became bad at times, so vision was poor. When the heavy rains fell out of the sky, it left large pools of dirty water, which made for terrible driving conditions. This made the convoy slow up a bit, but when the warm sun came out, the drivers made up for lost time. We still had not been told about where we were going, but all the soldiers had the feeling that the time for action was near. It was nearly nightfall as the lorries passed through another small town and, having been living near the sea, I knew we were approaching the ocean. I could smell the freshness in the air. The line of vehicles drew to a halt at the side of a quiet road. As we got off the lorries, we could see the mighty expanse of sea.

The soldiers formed into groups as they got down from their vehicles and waited to be told where we were and what to do next.

From a loud speaker, a very loud, gruff voice was heard. 'Now, listen to what I say and I will only say it once!' A moment of silence, then again the voice spoke. 'The landing crafts are not quite ready to transport all of you to your ships, so in the meantime please do not stray or wander away from the company you belong to and be prepared at a minute's notice to reload the crafts. Thank you.'

Time seemed to drag on and looking overhead I could see the hazy clouds floating over a yellow-coated moon, a sure sign that the weather was to change for the worse. I strolled down to stand beside the ocean and gazed out at the many ships moored in the bay. Even though it was quite dark, I could still see the huge nets strung along the entire length of the ships and thought to myself, surely they wouldn't expect anybody to climb this daft obstacle. I was completely wrong, as it happened. They did.

The chaplain was a very busy man at this time. He was consoling two men who were sobbing and clutching him, as if somehow he could save them. This incident made me feel very uneasy but, before I was able to think more about it, the order came for all men to board the landing crafts (LSTs).

There were about fifty men to each craft as they were loaded, and pushed away from the beach, to slowly make their way to a ship. Then all the soldiers climbed up the netting and on to the deck of the vessel. After all the men had settled on deck, the LSTs were hoisted up to lie along the side of the great vessel. Every man had to know where the craft he came on was located for, when we reached the other side of the Channel, he would be able to get in the same craft. At long last, all the men had got on board but space-wise there was not a lot of leg room. Our thoughts were interrupted by a very loud, stern voice that came over the intercom and it was no surprise that all the talking ceased for everyone was waiting to hear the news and receive their orders.

We had tried once before to weigh anchor and proceed to our destination, but bad weather stopped us from doing so. We also had a few words from High Command, who told us that now was the time to resume. For a few moments he ceased talking and then carried on. 'All the ship's personnel have worked very hard just to help you perform the duty you are about to undertake.' The voice ceased for a few moments, and then said, 'What I am about to say is of the utmost importance and, with hand on heart, I cannot say you are going on a picnic, but I, with the Padre's blessings, wish everyone of you good luck and an easy landing.'

I believe we all thought that this was the end of the message but the voice spoke out again, only this time it was very stern. 'From this time forth, there will be no loud noises, and especially naked lights, when our ship pulls up anchor. If anyone is reported going against my orders he will be put on charge and be harshly punished.' A pause, then the voice resumed. 'This is all I have to say but once again I wish you good luck and God go with you all.' These were soundly spoken words but I think everyone knew where we were heading and so it came as no surprise to hear that message.

The D-Day Landings

The account of the next 28 days is a collection of incidents and experiences that were so unbelievably ghastly that those who survived had nightmares for the rest of their lives. If there is a kingdom of hell, then I was about to walk through it. Never can I forget what we were ordered to do, but in no way could I, or my mates, refuse to do our duty. To turn back would have been cowardly and, anyway, the waters of the English Channel prevented us from doing so.

At around midnight that evening, the large troop ship pulled anchor and ever so slowly moved from its berth. The huge ship hardly made a sound as it moved away from the land and crept into the wide, dark Channel water. Above us the sky was overcast but occasionally we could see the odd star glittering through the breaks in the cloud. The whole vessel seemed to reflect an omen of bleak disaster, for everyone on this ship had no doubt that terrible trouble lay before us. I do not want you to think I was not affected by all that was going on around me, but on that night I did something I had never done before… I knelt down and, facing the cold water, I prayed. I really believe my prayers were answered, otherwise I certainly would not be here today.

A few of my friends were talking very quietly close beside me and across from me stood a solitary soldier staring at the sky. There was naked fear in his eyes. I recall walking over and laying my arm across his shoulder, 'Do you believe in God?' I asked.

He turned to face me and replied, 'Do you?' and then turned away. I tapped him on the arm and again he turned to face me and looked annoyed.

'Just about now, my friend, I hope to heaven there is and I also hope that no matter what happens we all will come through this ordeal and have a laugh about it later.' This I am sure did not take the fear from his eyes for, as he turned about to walk away, I could still see the ugly fear still on his face and there were just the beginning of tears forming in his eyes. This also upset me as I left him to walk along the deck of the large ship and look overhead at the star studded night sky.

There seemed to be stress all over the troop vessel and, although strong men are not supposed to cry, I could hear sobbing here and there and occasionally sounds of troops talking to themselves. I was scared and had asked myself many times 'Why am I here?' – but there was just no proper answer to this question. I also remembered the old saying 'fear begets fear'. There was not a young soldier aboard the ship that could honestly say he was not afraid, but there was the odd soldier putting on a bold front and we all knew these men were always the first to run away. My young friends and I all had different views about this war but we all agreed that somehow we were in the wrong war zone, but these decisions were not up to us.

In the early hours of 6 June 1944, the mighty engines of the troop liner became silent and all was as quiet as a graveyard. Everyone on the ship stopped what they were about to do and gazed long and hard at each soldier friend, knowing full well the time had come. The chaplain had come this far with us and had a grey book in his hands, which I presumed was the Bible. He was looking above him and saying something but I knew not what. I rose to my feet and peered over the iron railings of the vessel and could just make out the dark French shoreline. Above our quiet craft the sky looked very hazy and the odd stars, instead of being dim, were a dull red, but worst of all the ship was also being tossed about like a cork in a bottle.

No words were uttered over the loudspeakers but as the sergeant of Company A arose, we all got up to follow him. I, in my haste to keep up with the soldiers, dropped my light shoulder pack and had to find it in the dull light. Having secured it, I made my way to where the LST was. As it had already been lowered into the sea I had to sling myself over the side of the ship, grab the netting and climb down into the landing craft. I definitely would have been in the front of the landing craft but, as I was the last on board, I had to kneel down in the stern. The only noise I heard that night was the occasional rubbing of cloth against the metal sides and the very heavy breathing of the soldiers as they kneeled down. All the LSTs were in the sea, spread all along the side of the ship. How many, it would be impossible to say, for not only had our ship lowered landing craft, but the many ships all around us were doing the same.

Instead of being comfortable in the LST, all the men were being tossed from one position to another by the rough sea. A mile away from the coastline, all the great ships had moored and, as each of the landing crafts was loaded with men, they were being pushed away from the mother ships to travel, as we were, toward and alongside the shoreline. At long last, in the far distance we could just make out a sandy beach and every yard we went seemed to be a bonus. Then we got to thinking this was an easy 'walk-ashore' exercise.

The Omaha Beach landing on D-Day cannot be put into words. I believe it is like asking a man who walked through hell to describe the walk. Believe me, the words I use to tell of the landing and some of the battles will not tell you of the stress all us young men went through fighting this damn bloody war.

Every landing craft went straight toward land and then, when we got closer, we turned to run parallel to the coastline. Five or six hundred yards off the beach and about a mile later, the LST swung a little closer to the rocky coastline. This was to get away from the stiff sea breeze blowing from inland and, the sea did become less choppy. As I looked over the side of the boat, I could just make out on the skyline three large, black poles pointing skywards, and remember thinking, good job they are not guns of the German artillery. Quite a few of the landing craft were further out than ours, then they gradually swung around to go toward the shore but kept well spaced apart. We rounded a point of land and saw a long, sandy beach just to the right of us and again we thought it was to be an easy landing but we were wrong on all counts.

First the soldiers heard machine gun and then rifle fire but it was not directed at our landing craft, for we were out of range. About seven hundred yards from the sands we saw, to our dismay, the tragedy taking place concerning the first wave of craft that were heading towards the beach, half had turned over! Honest to God, there were just the black shapes of dead bodies almost everywhere. The army command was wrong, of course, in their intelligence; wrong, in fact, on all counts. The higher-ups did not have vital information about the Germans doing exercises in this area. (I only found out about this later.) The navy had fired their great guns at this beach to create shell holes on the sandy shore but the shells they fired went above and over the fortified beach and landed half a mile inland.

On this Omaha beachhead landing, we had drawn the short straw. The enemy were prepared and waiting for us and, as the cold, damp mist lifted, we were sitting ducks. The German troops had already foiled the first wave of the invasion on this beach and were quite ready to destroy as many LSTs as possible to prevent us taking this beachhead and it seemed, at the time, they were keeping us at bay. Upturned landing boats and bodies were floating in the red sea and still the craft I was in and all the other boats were making for the sands.

The young soldiers in the LST crouching in front of me knew we would be well within range very soon. While all this slaughter was going on, bullets were hitting the water beside us. I bet there was not a man in the LST boat who would have carried on after seeing what the first wave had gone through, but where in hell could we go? Only forward. To clarify, a landing craft was a very large, flat-bottomed boat that could carry tanks as well as soldiers. Unlike an ordinary boat, the whole front was able to fall forward and down, leaving a sort of ramp to drive or walk from.

As the haze cleared, the German gunners fired everything at us but the kitchen sink. Two of the LST boats to the right of us were blown completely out of the water, leaving debris and parts of bodies floating in the calm sea.

Shells were hitting craft everywhere and, although the morning sun was very bright, we could see the haze of smoke as one of the landing craft floated in flames just above the water. All this time we were getting closer to the brown-white sands and I could make out barbed wire and sea defences. On the wire was something white – it was a ragged piece of cloth, swinging back and forth in the sea breeze. We were that close to it that I could hear the hissing noise as the sea ran through the uprights holding the wire in place and then suddenly the young man just in front of me fell over the side into the sea with blood everywhere.

The boat was close to the wire, another two or three yards and the craft would have touched it. Then the gunners on shore homed in on us but at first the machine guns did not put us in any danger, for the gun bullets could not penetrate the hull, but when the heavy artillery joined in, we had no chance at all, for the very front of the landing craft blew backwards, disappearing and killing every soldier sitting in front. With more than half of my buddies dead, and the boat sinking, everyone was trying to save themselves from the blood-red sea. If I had been sooner rather than later boarding the large landing craft, I would have been sitting in the front and not be here to tell this story. The boat, as it broke in half, flattened the barbed wire, leaving me in the water up to my neck with about fifteen or twenty of my soldier friends.

Splashing around and pushing a piece of wood away, I was just able to touch the bottom of the sea, but only on tiptoes and I had also lost my rifle. There were about a dozen of us who had survived and somehow made it to the waterline. Even this had to be done with great care, for the machine gunners were having a wonderful day. The few soldiers that had survived wiggled like long sea snakes out of the water to lie between the dead bodies, washed up by the crimson sea.

Many minutes I lay there and then I felt something brushing against my leg. I turned and, looking down, saw a dead young soldier about my age who was staring at me with sightless eyes. I remember reaching down and closing them with my fingers. At the same time I looked at the enemy line and yelled, 'You goddamn son of a bitch!' There was many a time I could have been killed during the war and each time I was lucky, and sometimes, I swear to God, I saw my mother's dad moving his arms in a 'take it easy' fashion. Maybe it was my imagination, but I still think today he was with me when I needed help.

I lay amongst the dead, in fact, I played dead. It didn't take too much working out what the goddamn machine gunners were doing. As each craft approached the sands the front would go down and so the gunner would machine gun the boat, slaying nearly everyone on the landing craft. As this was happening, the few soldier friends with me crawled and slithered along the sands towards the shoreline.

At long last, about a dozen of us were concealed behind the triangular sea defence and well hidden. There was an art to making our way to safety, we found out the hard way. Every time the machine gunner fired rounds over us, we stopped moving and we tried to lay close to a dead soldier but this did not work all the time, for occasionally a man would die, but quite a few of us reached safety. Looking back to the beach, we could see wave after wave of LSTs still unloading men and there were dead soldiers everywhere, but for every man who died, there was yet another taking his place.

We also knew that no soldier could stop to help his buddy, as this would surely imperil his own life. On my way to this place of refuge, I had picked up another rifle – believe me they were very easy to come by. All types of firearms were here, even rocket grenades. I could remember the command the troops had received before the landing: 'do not take any prisoners'. Sitting behind the wooden triangle, it began to look as if no one would be around to take any!

All day long we were held beside this beach and suffered casualties of all types. I gazed at the men around me and touched something wet on my left leg. Looking down at my hand it was covered in blood and just below my knee cap blood was oozing through my trousers. Taking a closer look, the wound was only minor, so, ripping a piece of the cloth from the barbed wire, I wrapped it tightly around the open gash. Looking back and along the coast, I knew how lucky the group around me were, for all one could hear were cries for help and yells of severe pain.

I found the ones who were in charge were the first to die during the landing at Omaha. The ironic thing about this was that they taught the whole company the art of survival and yet they became the first casualties. Because of this, the majority of survivors were left without a real leader. I suppose nobody ever thought this would ever happen and so took it for granted that someone would be around to lead us but, as it had happened, everyone had to use his own common sense to stay alive. I cannot say with any real certainty that all the officers had perished on the beachhead landing but I do know the captain and two sergeants had never left the landing craft – they had all perished when a shell struck the front of the boat. I knew every one of those brave men. The explosion was so great they vanished before my eyes and I have never seen the sea water so red.

All along the beach the triangular structures had more and more men hiding behind them but for every soldier concealed behind the wooden framework, there were an uncountable number lying dead upon the sands. Above my hiding place there was a large mound of earth that was jutting out from the land but hidden by many bushes. Almost in front of these leafy clumps but just below them ran a long, stony path with a single fence, running parallel to the shoreline, presumably used as a defence for the bunkers.

A large group of men had congregated just behind the two wooden triangles. Only a stone's throw away were the enemy lines, and believe me, we were lucky to be here, considering the heavy machine gun fire that was coming from the Germans. At that precise moment in time, I saw something that nobody else had seen and pointed it out to my buddies. Each time the breeze blew, it parted some of the green foliage of the large bushes and I could see the shape of a German sitting behind a large machine gun. Although we could not see the gun crew; we did know they would be very close by.

Maybe, just maybe, if we took this gun out of action then we could gain a foothold in the enemy lines. At least if we took this gun out it would stop a lot of the bloodshed. The risk was worth taking, for every minute we stayed on these sands the enemy kept on killing our men. A young soldier was chosen to try to contact every one of the men concealed behind the high wooden structures and the order was that when the machine gun noise from this part of the beach ceased, then everyone close to this area would attempt to cross the enemy line.

Three men lay on the dry sands with rifles aimed at the large bush and another three lay just behind them with hand grenades in their hands. All at once the bushes parted, a rifle shot rang out, and the gunner was seen to fall forward over the embankment. As the German was seen falling, all the hand grenades were thrown above the dry bushes. As this happened, the young soldiers leapt forward and quite a few of my friends were killed but I do believe the German did not know we were that close.

We were so near to the enemy that it came down to hand-to-hand combat and we certainly had our hands full. I do not want you to think that the small group of soldiers I was with had solely made it possible for our division to get a toehold on enemy lines. Other groups were also figuring out how to take this stronghold without losing too many men. The men in the small group I was with knew that now more and more men would breach the open stronghold and join us. We American soldiers were so enraged by the killing of so many of our men that we began fighting like demons. I cannot be expected to remember every detail of this battle because I was too busy trying to stay alive.

That same day, I found out what it felt like to stare another man in the eyes and kill him. I know, whilst fighting, one hasn't the time to think about this, for he is too busy trying to stay alive himself. Later, though, all the horrors return and stay with him for the rest of his life. I just keep reminding myself that over four thousand young GIs were left on this beach, wounded or dead, so it was a small consolation that we slew a few of the enemy.

Whilst I was busy fighting a German, I saw one of my buddies open a bunker door and throw a hand grenade inside, shutting the door as he did so. The loud noise of the explosion probably saved my life, for whilst I was being held by the throat by a very tall Nazi, another German was about to bayonet me in the back. To this day I cannot remember exactly how I did it, but I quickly turned and the German turned with me. Instead of me getting the bayonet, the German received it. I will never forget the look on his face and the scream as he fell to the ground just beside me.

The large breach of the enemy line had gone some way to stopping the slaughter of the waves of men coming ashore. This also gave the medics (God bless them) the chance to tend to the wounded. To this day, I cannot understand why we began to take prisoners but just maybe it was because everyone had seen so much death and was fed up with killing. Nevertheless, the more ground we secured, the less reason we had to seek revenge. Looking back to the battles I was in, this was the only time there were no military police involved, at least not in this place of action.

In all of my fighting days, I never asked for forgiveness, only to stay alive and to be protected from all harm. In later life, I asked God to forgive me for all those I had slain, even though it was a case of kill or be killed. I recall the last hand-to-hand combat I engaged in before the fortified beach was taken. Around a bend, in a large grey-stoned passage way, I had come across a very tall German. He had an ugly smile on his face and we were both taken by surprise. At that time I sure as hell thought I was a goner. We both aimed and pulled our triggers but all we heard was a dull click, for both of us had empty rifles. I had a feeling he would be faster than me reloading his rifle, as his only took one shell.

I did the only thing I could do to beat him. I stood the rifle bayonet upright on the hard, cold earth, pulled the bayonet from the rifle and threw it with all my might. Even today I can see the look of surprise on his face for the knife went into his shoulder up to the hilt, and in a way I was feeling really thankful, for it was not meant to be a killing throw. I had no time to feel guilty because the killing on the beach was still going on, but gradually it seemed to be coming to an end. The Germans were becoming fewer and fewer and were retreating to the rear as they were pushed to the back.

What we did not understand was why our troops had seen no Tiger tanks and the lack of the panzer division. If they had been in the conflict we probably would have lost even more men and maybe the beachhead as well. Looking behind and to the right of where I was standing, everywhere seemed to look like an unburied cemetery, because bodies and parts of them were strewn everywhere. The last three hand grenades were thrown and at long last the beach was captured and the few prisoners taken at the end of the battle were standing in a line and looking really downhearted.

Most of the US soldiers, as they left to go slowly inland just raised two fingers. In our hearts we all knew there should not have been a prisoner taken alive because the enemy must have slain thousands of American soldiers and here they were walking free, to be sent back as prisoners of war, to live a life of luxury for the rest of the damn war, probably somewhere in good old Yankee Land.

There was not one soldier among the company who wasn't dirty, tired and stressed. Two full days had gone by without enough sleep, food or any comfort, and I wondered what had brought us through this hell we had faced. Greenhorns to veterans in two days – not bad considering that most of the men were still only in their teens. The whole company went nearly two miles inland, well away from the beach, before we found a safe place to settle for the night.

This was in a field surrounded by tall hedgerows. In fact, much of Normandy was farmland and everywhere one looked there were these barriers with usually one wooden gate for an entrance. These were used mostly for cows and horses but the one we chose had no animals in it. Sentries were posted for there was always the chance of a counterattack as so many Germans had fled the beach.

A new captain had just taken charge of Company A and, with his permission, we all fell out to find a place to rest. As the new supplies of C-rations turned up, we ate them, with a small tin of meat as well. The trickle of blood started to ooze from my leg again, so I poured water from my canteen over the open gash, wiping it clean with a piece of cloth, and redressed it. I also took my helmet off. With wonder and amazement, I looked at the jagged hole a missile had made in my helmet. I never recalled being shot but whatever it was must have hit the upper part of my helmet and if it had gone just an inch lower I would not be alive to tell this tale.

Having made myself a place to rest, I leaned back against a large tree and was soon fast asleep.

I don't know how long I slept that night but it was just as well that someone nudged me awake for I was having nightmares. I opened my eyes and saw my old friend, Stobs, and he was pointing to Sergeant Bowchamp in the murky background. He had worked as cook before we were in combat – now he was a front-line soldier. I suppose it was unfair, for he had not been on route marches or taken part in any of the endurance tests. How the man had survived the beach landing I will never know, but I suppose the same could be said of me!

The sun had appeared quite early that morning and, whilst I had been asleep, the sergeant had been looking around the area for something to eat.

He eventually made a quick grab at something we couldn't see and then we saw the red feathers. The rooster never stood a chance but just how the dickens would he cook it? I do believe he had already worked it out but first he had to slay and pluck it. The killing was quite easy and even the plucking presented no problems, so what would he do now? Well, he already had a bundle of wood on the ground and before long the fire was alight.

Then, he surprised us. Taking his canteen, he poured the water from it into his helmet, then he put the rooster inside it, and then put his helmet on to the fire.

Suddenly, the sound of a rifle could be heard to the right of me, and we all glanced that way, momentarily losing interest in what the sergeant was doing, but almost instantly looked back again. He had just raised the bird into the air and, shouting with glee, ripped off one of its barely cooked legs. He was putting it into his open mouth, when another shot was heard. He fell on to the fire, spilling the water from his iron helmet and everyone could see the look of utter amazement on his face. The sniper that killed him was in the opposite field, almost hidden to us by the green leafed tree.

The sniper more than likely would have got away with it but a large blackbird had flown from the tree at the sound of gunfire, so it was obvious where the shot had come from. There could have been at least twenty men shooting at this sniper and, as he fell from the tree, he must have had at least twelve pounds of lead in him. This incident made us aware of snipers and the need to stay alert at all times.

There was no more resting for anyone, so we all formed groups, collected our rations for the day and were soon back on the move. Sometime later, a farmhouse was seen in the distance and a long, winding dusty road was running beside it. As the squad drew closer to the house, it looked ancient and had a thatched roof, which was something I had never seen before. The ground was very muddy – it had been raining heavily for some time – and this was where I saw my first dead civilian.

The corpse of a short woman lay half in and half out of a huge, muddy puddle. As for her age, I could only guess, for a tank had run over her head and the smell of death was almost everywhere. Horses and cows lay bloated, some in the road and some beside it. We even passed the odd pig. With the animals and the dead woman, the air made everyone feel quite sick.

All of us gave a great sigh of relief as we passed through and out of the walled yard. We pushed forward, walking through field after field. The odd man or woman was seen slowly running along the very wet, muddy road, sometimes smiling but more often than not waving their hands and even bowing as the line of men went past. There was the odd occasion when a person would offer a bottle of brandy to one of the soldiers which meant that several would be stumbling or hobbling along, drunk.

To the left and right of my own position I saw the long line of young men all walking forward, but each of the soldiers were at least one or two hundred yards apart, stopping occasionally to search for the enemy. It had been just a quiet, tiring, normal day, which went to prove that the enemy was somewhere ahead.

About two miles ahead, we saw seven men run across a big field and, even from that distance, I could see they were carrying a large object, which I made out to be a gun. I then saw two other men follow and, a short time later, a volley of gunfire rang out.

I ran across two fields and slowed right down at the third, for this was where I had seen the seven men. At that time I was not able to tell if they were Germans or my friends, so stooping over and following the huge hedgerow, I crawled along its side.

I stopped when I came to the large lopsided gate and peered around. Again, I thank my lucky stars... if I had taken a step or walked around and into the field, I most certainly would have died. In the field but lying almost on top of each other, I could see two dead soldiers and beside them a third dead man was laying, with wide open, sightless eyes. They were the BAR men (manning a large semi-automatic rifle on a tripod) and so they must have been the soldiers we all had seen in the distance. All three men were facing me. One man's helmet had been torn from his head where a lead bullet had struck him. I remember all this vividly, as I knew these men very well. I could also see the gold watch the head gunner was wearing. His name, curiously, was Ralph America!

Slowly standing up beside a tree stump that protruded just above the hedge, I was able to see a grass-topped pillbox. The box was so concealed by the grass that I understood why it had not been located and the reason why America and his two chums had died. As the three BAR men walked across the open-gated section of the hedgerow, they became sitting ducks for the machine gunners sitting in the pillbox. I made sure no one was alive by calling out their names. Getting no response, I sat down to ponder what to do about the men who had killed my friends. Then I had a brilliant idea. Maybe what I was about to do would not kill the bastards, but certainly they would feel the heat, and they probably would find it difficult to breath. Every regiment was given strict instructions never to use naked fire during the war and so the soldiers carried a special lighter. It had no flame but it did have a slow-burning wick.

So, making a torch out of dead grass and putting the wick and the grass together, I blew on the two and was able to set it alight. Then I chucked the torch as far as I could into the tall, dry grass around the pillbox, and to my delight, my plan worked out perfectly. In fact, too damn perfectly, for the whole area in the field burned so quickly I had only just enough time to get out the way I had come, before the entire field was alight. As I scurried out of the field, I heard an explosion where I had been, and often wonder today if the Germans fighting in that concrete pillbox survived.

Two fields later, I joined two of my buddies and, after exchanging a few words, we carried on to the next hedged field, which appeared to look quite peaceful. We were spread apart from each other but all at once a large explosion sounded to the left of me, followed by another and I stopped dead in my tracks. It did not take much figuring out that the three of us had entered a mine field and I was the only survivor. Dropping flat on the ground, I could not help but look to where the explosion had occurred and was not surprised to see body parts scattered everywhere. Overhead and out of the sky, specks of blood were falling to the ground.

I reached and withdrew the bayonet from my belt. Slightly digging it into the wet earth as I crawled forward, I found to my utter horror that if I had taken a step I also would have been just another dead veteran, for my bayonet found another landmine. It took a long time to crawl along the field but, after finding three more mines, I finally reached the old wooden gate of the hedged field and gave a sigh of relief as I climbed over the tall hedge and, believe it or not again, found I was a lucky man for as I dropped to the other side of the hedge, I noticed it had a booby trap. Lying on the other side, I brushed the sweat from my brow with my sleeve and lay in that position for a long time. In my heart, I felt nothing but sorrow for my dead soldier friends.

Making my way back to my platoon took quite some time and when I rejoined my company it was getting towards evening. I was so tired, my feet felt as if they were falling off and I had to put another bandage around the shrapnel wound on my left leg, for there was a slight trickle of blood forming again. I came to a small pebbled stream flowing under an old wooden bridge and decided that now was the time to have a quiet rest. As I was taking off my shoes, one of my buddies sat down beside me and said, 'Where the hell have you been all day?'

I looked at him in complete amazement and when I told him what I had done he said, 'Well, I'll be damned.'

We both sat and chatted for a spell, bathing our tired feet as we talked. A while later each of us took turns on sentry duty whilst the other slept. The company was staying here for the night so we dug a foxhole and gingerly crawled into it. I never knew the time but do know the hole was very comfortable and, even though I was lying in a puddle of water, I fell fast asleep.

When a soldier cannot talk or understand words in French or German, it is almost impossible to read signposts. Therefore, we knew we were fighting a war in France but to tell anyone the route my company was taking, I could not say. I knew, however, that we were not far from the coast and the soldiers were going towards a place signposted 'Cherbourg'.

Our entire company of soldiers were following a pathway along the side of a pine tree forest, walking and talking softly amongst ourselves, but before we knew it, there were shouts of alarm, for we had walked straight into an ambush. In front of us had once stood a fir tree but it had been blown into the air and had fallen on top of a squad of men. Realising we were victims of an ambush, we ran like hell. Then the shelling started. We went back quite a distance, all of us lying behind a huge ditch as the shelling continued. Then a while later the shelling stopped and we again formed an outward line and went back to see where the giant tree had fallen. The sergeant wanted to see if any of the soldiers missing from our unit were still alive. The whole area where we had been had large holes in the earth and fallen trees lay everywhere. We found Corporal Stone and he was dead but there were no bullet marks on him. He had died under a big branch of the tree.

We pulled the dead pine branches away from the tree, revealing another three of our chums. I certainly will never forget the soldiers who died that day, for they were very good friends of mine and these men had been fighting with me since the landing at Omaha Beach. Again, they had died during the falling of the large tree. The fate of these brave men was pushed to the back of my mind, for if I had broken down at the death of every soldier I knew, I just would not have survived this terrible war.

Many times in the bloody battles I took part in, there always seemed to be one old building that was left untouched by the air bombing. The artillery only did minor damage to the buildings. These were the wonderful, old grey-stone churches, standing defiantly alone, whilst other buildings fell down around them. This was a wonderful sight to behold but the enemy also took advantage of these sacred places by using them as ambush centres.

As the days went by, I seemed to get less and less sleep. Added to this was the lack of food and chances to bathe. And, with death all around me, I began to have really bad nightmares.

One morning after, the company awoke and gathered together for orders. We then walked in a staggered line, 500 yards apart, until we saw the dark blue of the ocean and then followed the coastline for quite a while to veer inland.

The day seemed very peaceful, hardly a sound was heard except in the distance, I could just make out the odd, grey silhouette of men running here and there and to the right of the hill stood a dry, old thatched building. I rushed forward to tell the captain what had been seen. He immediately took a field phone to report to the top brass the situation but as he was phoning all hell broke loose. The first shell hit and exploded about fifty yards to my left, then another a bit closer to where we stood.

Having been in this situation before, I started to run, as did the rest of the platoon. We then started to dig foxholes and very deep trenches, to move to where the enemy could not see us. Everyone on hand knew where the danger lay – it was coming from the huge building – but we could not capture or destroy it without outside help. We were saved from being hurt because the officer had put a phone message through, informing them about the building. A short time later, the old house was no more, for a barrage of artillery shells hit it. The old wooden building broke up and parts of it flew everywhere.

This, however, did not cause the shelling to stop but now the American artillery was going over everyone's heads and the enemy shells were doing the same – they both were trying to silence each other. This gave our men time to get out of our holes and, following each other, we ran like hell across the field to the left of us and up a small, dry dirt road to find shelter from these big guns. That afternoon we got a message from our headquarters ordering us to halt the forward march we were on and find a place of safety to wait for further orders. The company was broken up and every soldier found a comfortable place to relax.

This also gave us time to take off our heavy boots and have a good rest. A short time later we were told to dig in, for we would be staying here for a short while. We dug out deep foxholes but some of the men were so tired that they dug slit trenches instead. The rough, dry earth where the platoon rested was as hard as red brick but at last I was satisfied about the depth. Putting my small pack spade away, I rolled into it and was able to sit and look out of the top. I was tired when I started to dig and when I had finished I closed my eyes and fell into a deep sleep.

Not long after, I was woken by a slight vibration in the ground. Rolling on to my side, I was able to glance out of my sleeping place, only to roll back in again. To my amazement, I saw two panzer tanks almost on top of me. One of the Tiger tanks started to fire at my chums. I actually looked out the top of my hole and glanced up at the side of the giant tank.

I rolled over then lay dead still as the large muddy tank drove over the top of my hole. As it went over the top I could have reached up and touched the bottom. The tank going over me proved just how hard the soil was and I stayed put for a long while before coming out of the hole.

The big tanks had long gone and, in leaving, had blown holes in the earth everywhere, but what annoyed me more than anything was that we were not warned beforehand. As before, we all gathered again to reform the line and then walk up a long, dusty road.

As we were going along, just beyond us, an artillery barrage was being fought out and, as we were walking, the German .88s were going over the top of us. From the other direction came the Americans big .155 mm artillery shells (nicknamed 'the whispering death'). They seemed to land about a mile either side of us. Walking up a hill, weary and not expecting anything to happen, a German ran across the old dirt road about 500 yards in front of the man leading our platoon.

I'd bet nearly everyone tramping up the road fired their rifle at him but, believe it or not, not a single bullet hit him. In fact, I can still remember seeing him throw himself into the dark undergrowth at the side of the road. I think this made everyone angry. Then the man halted, turned and, as he vanished, put two fingers up.

It had been a funny old day with the tanks and then that very, very lucky German, but the day was now coming to a close, so all the soldiers drew up alongside the road to find another place to spend the night and make plans for the coming day.

Every time the bright, hot sun passed over the horizon and the pale yellow moon rose to bathe the earth in shadows, it became time to thank the Good Lord for another day. I soon fell into a deep sleep.

Front-line Action

On this warm, dark night, our sergeant made a horrible mistake. It was one that would claim the lives of four of the men in the platoon. I suppose owing to being tired, he forgot a very important code that everyone had learned in basic training… to always protect your rear flank. He forgot about putting out the sentries. Waking a few times during the night, I could hear the odd snore coming from the foxhole just beside my own, but I took no notice of this. I just stretched my legs, rolled over and went to sleep. When I awoke early the following morning, there was lots of shouting and I saw two soldiers looking down into the foxhole just beside mine. The two men looked very angry and stressed, and one of them was shaking his fist in the air. The man was in tears and was calling out the names of the men in the hole. Another soldier came to stand just beside him. As he looked he shouted over and over again, 'The dirty bastards!' and, raising his rifle in the air, kept firing until he had used up all the shells.

All of us looked to see if the sentry had survived and then was told no one had been posted on duty that evening. At any other time, a soldier would have been put on charge for this stupid mistake but being in enemy territory they deemed it just another error of judgement. So the main officer in charge had learned a very costly lesson and I do know it never happened again. We found out later, from a prisoner of war, that a German patrol had passed that way during the night and finding no one on lookout was a gift from the gods that they took with both hands. All four of the soldiers were bayoneted whilst they slept but I did not realise until later that day that my foxhole was next in line and I often wonder why the Jerries did not carry on slaughtering their easy victims.

My God, didn't I have a humdinger of a headache and I felt very low in spirit, so I sat down, closed my eyes, and leaned back against a tree to relieve the pain in my head. Before I knew it, I was thinking of the past and the day I earned my promotion.

I got it as a result of an event that happened a short time after D-Day, my buddy Paul (a fellow private) and I were out in front of our platoon, scouting, and were in front by about six hundred yards, but always on the alert, ready for anything. Everything was going according to plan and we were approaching a large field with the usual hedges. I took a long stride, looked to my right and, as I did so, there was a loud explosion and I saw my friend fly up into the air. I flung myself to the ground, Paul screamed and then there was complete silence. Without a doubt, I knew what had just happened. He had stepped on a landmine and his left foot had been blown off.

The platoon behind us had all thrown themselves to the soft, muddy ground and were shooting at the opposite hedge. As this was going on, I was able to get close enough to Paul to grab him and pull him towards me. He was in a serious condition, blood was everywhere and it somehow had to be stopped from flowing out of his body. I had nothing to make a tourniquet with but, as it happened, Paul's boot was very close by and I was able to take the lace from it and quickly wind it around the pressure point on his leg.

This partially stopped the flow of blood but I knew he needed help urgently. Without a thought for myself, I leaned over and hoisted the now unconscious man on to my shoulder. Fortunately, he wasn't too heavy. I started back the way I came very carefully. No one shot at us, maybe they were waiting for me to step on another landmine. Luckily, I didn't!

Somehow, I did reach the medics, and they carried poor Paul away and, although I was then upgraded to corporal, I still would have preferred my friend's company to the extra stripe!

The weather had turned misty, damp and windy but once the company regrouped to go forward, the rain started to pour down, worsening as the day wore on. We had no proper rainwear, so we got soaked to the skin. We were all tired and fed up with this damn war.

An hour later the rain abated, leaving a slight drizzle, but it was still misty. We all saw the trees on the horizon and the whole platoon walked very slowly towards them, hoping to find shelter from the elements. About one hundred yards from the woods, the man on my left fell to the ground as a rifle shot was heard. There were four of us scouting that rainswept day, and the three of us that remained flung ourselves to the ground. Suddenly, machine gun and rifle bullets were going just over our heads and many of them were hitting the company of men following behind us, and this meant casualties. Men began to scream and others tried to find some type of cover in order to return the rifle fire. It was like shooting at dark shadows and, while this went on, the company could not go forward or retreat.

We scouts were nearer to the forest's edge than the main group of soldiers, so we quickly pushed, slithered, and crawled to the outskirts of the trees and lay with our backs to the odd stumps of the pines. Looking back from where we all lay, we could see the many dark shapes of bodies that lay on the earth. Many were still firing towards the trees. I am sure they could not see anything. It was a hopeless task. This was almost as bad as the Omaha landing, for we were again sitting ducks. We prayed for a miracle.

We three were kneeling under the tree in a pool of wet, cold and slimy mud and coming from the next field we heard a very loud humming noise. Then, in the distance, we could just make out the shape of a huge tank. As it was coming up the long, wet road, we at first thought it was a panzer, but as it got closer, we saw it was one of ours, a Sherman. Its turret kept moving from left to right and, beside this one, another appeared. In all, we counted four. Our prayers had been answered! All of the tanks came through the space between the huge hedgerows, pushing down and running over an old, wooden fence as they did so. Then they all came to a stop, facing the woods. The turrets all swung to the left, then all the big guns began firing. I thanked my lucky stars they were not pointing my way, but they were near enough for the odd shell to blow debris over our place of concealment.

One foolish German came from the woods to aim an anti-tank shell at the Shermans but he didn't stand a chance, for just as he emerged from concealment one of the shells hit him and he just disappeared. All at once the noise of firing ceased. The enemy drew back into the undergrowth. As we were so close to them, we got to our feet and began to follow them. The Sherman tanks had certainly changed this ugly situation, for instead of being on the receiving end, we were dishing it out!

The afternoon was nearly gone when everyone entered the undergrowth to leave the good old medics to tend to the sick and dying. No resistance was met, as the Germans had drawn all their troops back, leaving an empty forest, with just the odd sniper to contend with.

Many a good man had died that day and there was no holding back those who wanted to get revenge on the German soldiers who had carried out the ambush. However, it was not a big forest, just a small tract of trees and it was not too long before we came out the other side of the wood.

We were amazed to find some of the Germans with their hands above their heads and waving a white piece of cloth frantically in the air. This was not a particularly popular outcome. Not all the Germans gave up during the battle, for many of them went across the next field to disappear and fight again. The vast majority of those men were from the old guard, the SS, the hardcore of the German army.

The American army soldiers had lost very close friends on that day, but this had happened in all battles, from the beachhead landings up to the present time and all of us knew that one day it could be us but, to be truthful, we were too damn tired to care. We would leave this battle ground with just another memory, but in the meantime, we had at least another three quarters of Normandy to walk through. Now that this battle was over and had quietened down, we had to count our losses and find a place to settle for the night.

The following morning we got up to stand in a small group to receive our orders for the day. My group of five scouts went walking along a large valley towards a high field that stood in the distance. I was scouting in the lead for about two miles and beckoned the other four scouts to follow the route along the lower ground. As they did that, I scouted on the side of the grassy hill almost to the top. I found this worked out very well, for I could see the four at the bottom and, as they would inspect the bottom, I would be able to see everything at the top. Nothing unusual occurred until we reached the end of the valley and, as I was above and leading quite a distance in front, I observed the large old building first.

The four at the bottom of the valley were not able to see it, and neither did they realise a group of Germans could see them all approaching, for they had scurried into the house to await their arrival. No way could I warn them as it would have put me in jeopardy. I had hardly any time to make a decision but in a flash it came to me to attack the house. I had six full clips of ammunition (each clip held twelve bullets) and in each clip I put a tracer bullet (not an ordinary bullet but a bullet that looked like a spark as it travelled toward its target), then a live shell. Lying on the hard ground, I aimed at a top window and fired a tracer bullet. The noise of the rifle, and seeing the spark of the tracer on the way to the building, made the four at the bottom of the slope immediately stop and look up, and quickly throw themselves to the earth.

The tracer bullet acted as an arrow, pointing out where I was to fire the next shot. Then a live shell was fired and as I fired the second tracer, I could see each round fired was going into the old upstairs room. Then I fired the whole clip of bullets, reloaded and kept on firing tracers into the open space until smoke came billowing out of the window and I knew for certain that the upstairs room was on fire. Waiting for a short time, I then saw the flames and what I had expected happened... the German soldiers somewhere inside were in for a surprise.

While I was setting the building ablaze, the scouts below me had hidden themselves behind three trees that stood near the house. The next few minutes were nerve-wracking for I could not be sure that the Jerries had remained in the confines of the madly blazing building. All of them could have gone to the other side and maybe were hiding in other parts of the huge garden. The fire was coming out of the doorway of the house. I was able to see the fire inside the upstairs window burning furiously and I could hear the sounds of falling timber.

I got to my feet and, very slowly, made my way down the hill, skirting a large bush and was just in time to hear the Germans as they jumped out of a window, shooting at anything that moved. They gunned down one of the scouts who showed himself but the Germans never stood a chance. It was a gamble on their part but we held all the aces. The whole battle was over in about twenty minutes, leaving on the earth six very dead Germans.

It was the toss of a coin that decided the fate of the seventh man, whom we took prisoner. This man turned out to be a high-ranking officer and he was taken under guard to the nearest holding headquarters without delay. Quite a while later, all of us scouts were congratulated for outstanding bravery.

The enemy's front line was about two miles in front of us, so we had to be extremely careful. To avoid being a victim of snipers, the platoon would always spread out in a long line with at least three or four hundred yards between each other.

There was never a dull moment and it was very rare for the platoon to have a quiet night's sleep. As a scout, I would have the odd mission to carry out. One of those short rests came to an end as a high-ranking officer sitting near bushes yelled, 'You lot,' as he pointed at the platoon. 'Come around me and go forward and keep your tails to the ground, very soon each of you will see action.' He had not mentioned how far away it would be, but there was only one way to go and that was forward.

Three of us decided to stay as close as possible together but not to stay in a group. The rest of the platoon carried straight on and my chums and I veered slightly to the left, to find that we were quite a distance in front of the main line of troops. This meant we were leaving the main part of the platoon behind. As we took up the task of scouting our way into and among the hedged fields to finally reach the bottom of the steep hill, an old house came into view. Private Lazar pointed to a huge grey rock and the three of us sat behind it, to stare at the house with suspicion. It was situated in an isolated position and must have been miles from the nearest town. Then I sighted a flicker of a bright light appearing at an upstairs window. To make doubly sure of having seen it, I pointed it out to the others just as it began flickering again.

With guns at the ready we went slowly towards the old building but it became very difficult for us to conceal ourselves, for the bushes and trees were gradually thinning out. We then stopped to rest, quite a distance away, to sit upright against a boulder and just wait and watch. The dull, flickering light had gone out but started again, going on and off as if someone were sending a private message.

The three of us were in no doubt that this was being done in an attempt to point out the position of the American platoon. We waited in this place for quite a time until the flashing light stopped, and not long after this the platoon started to approach the old house but was ordered to go no further forward. We three scouts had reported what we had seen when we made our report to the commanding officer. To our dismay, he took no notice. Maybe it could be put down to tiredness, since everyone was exhausted after having a very busy day.

If the captain had taken the scouts' report and acted upon it, what happened next might not have taken place. I still believe the coded message by mirror from the window told the enemy exactly where we were and so they were prepared, waiting for our arrival. The German marksmen seemed everywhere, from a huge tree close by and from over the long stone wall. My friend Lazar beside me was one of the first casualties but he was lucky. The bullet that hit him went into his open mouth and came out of his cheekbone.

Another man walking beside him literally had his arm cut off by shrapnel and then the artillery barrage came in earnest. The damn Jerries inside the window had certainly done their job well, but to this day I still say the old house should have been taken out of action or at least been duly investigated. Just maybe this massacre could have been avoided but, of course, it became just another 'accident' by someone of unknown rank. There were other acts of stupidity during my twenty-eight days of battle for which the front-line soldier paid the price!

The heavy artillery guns of the .88s just threw everything at us and the bodies of my comrades were floating in the air around me. Somehow I survived without even a scratch and made a run to a big hole lying just under a hedge and jumped into it, just beating another tall soldier. The two of us filled the hole completely. In fact I could hardly breathe, he was so fat.

My guardian angel must have been with me. As we both leapt into the hole, a .88 shell hit the very top of the banking, blowing the man on top to pieces. The place of refuge we had jumped into was part of a cesspit and with the stench coming from below and the bloody remains on top of my body, I just could not move. I was petrified! Then I vaguely remember crying like a newborn, and if someone had just asked my name at that time, I would not have known it.

I do recall shoving the remains of my dead comrade off me and looking at the old house. I just could not believe it, for it was no longer there, only the foundation with debris everywhere. Two Sherman tanks appeared on the scene and, as the shelling ceased for a short while, I stumbled out of the area, with a bunch of soldiers following me. Coming to a small running stream of water, I threw myself in it without worrying about what I was wearing. In fact, I was so shell-shocked at that time, I did not know what I was doing.

I do, however, recall the soldiers passing by me, but it was a long time later before I got to my feet. God, what a headache I had. Even though I had jumped into the water, I still looked a mess, for my gear was still blood-stained but I very slowly limped along the way the platoon went, giving a small prayer of thanks. I believe I was literally speechless for at least three hours and kept thinking about what had happened. It was such a nightmare I had gone through!

The rest of the platoon had moved a considerable distance before we caught up with them and were very slowly approaching a small town. All the French buildings in the area seemed deserted and all I could hear was an animal howling in the distance. Everyone was on the alert as we very quickly spread apart to go cautiously from doorway to doorway to search each house for some kind of life. The odd Frenchman was found, but we never knew whether they were French or German until they spoke.

The platoon had made some good headway in finding and clearing the town of the enemy, but it was just the odd sniper that did the most damage to the platoon, for they had killed many young American soldiers as we were passing through the large town. Speaking quite candidly, we still were not sure that a few of the dead were not French snipers, because there were many a French collaborator fighting with the Germans during the war. Of course, this was to be expected as they had been under German occupation for many years.

We were relieved to get away from that town but there were many sad faces, for some soldiers had left good chums behind whom they would never see again.

Within a short time all the company had arrived at another town, only this was a lot larger than the one we had just liberated. This time there were quite a few people on the sidewalk. As we slowly walked along the road there were yells of welcome from many of the people, and even the odd drink was offered and although most of the men refused, the occasional unsteady gait made it obvious that some had taken advantage.

We were extremely lucky in gaining access to that town, for the Jerries had moved out just before we had arrived.

One thing was surely certain during the liberation of these old towns and villages as soon as we liberated these places the military police always moved in. The infantry units always came off second best, for if we had tried to return to the town we would have been shot. One thing I can recall as I walked through the town as we emerged from it, there was a long piece of wood nailed on a post and it had an arrow painted on it pointing to 'Saint-Lô'. This, of course, meant nothing to me, but we followed this sign for about five miles before splitting up to walk a distance apart. Every so often the company had to pull to the side of the long dirt road and wait patiently for new soldiers to take the place of the dead and wounded.

One day, whilst on scouting duty, I walked around a large bush and I saw a skinny, little man sitting in front of a large, brown boulder. He got up as I neared him and stood like a frightened man as I pointed my rifle at him. He uttered words in French that I just could not comprehend, then said, 'Comrade,' and pointed at me. 'Americano,' he said, then putting his hand in a pocket, he drew it out and held his skinny palm upward and to my amazement was holding a fist full of diamond rings.

I knew immediately where this pile of diamonds had come from and I nearly shot the bastard dead. It must have taken this skinny, little French man, hours to collect this loot from all the dead bodies. In a way, I also felt a little bit sorry for the man, because God only knows how long he had gone without food. I'm glad I never shot him. As he turned to run away, he dropped the rings and hurried out of sight. Even today, I sometimes wonder how I threw away a fortune, for I threw the lot over a hedgerow and then calmly walked away.

Miles in front, I stopped to sit down and decided to take my shoes and socks off and dangle them in a small stream flowing down a bank. God, what a relief it was. I almost fell into the stream as I shut my eyes for a while. After putting my shoes back on, I started to walk and arrived at a large old wood framed bridge. It was here I rejoined most of my platoon. Then we encountered another problem.

A team of mortar firers manned the area just opposite. The very first shell landed where the soldiers were walking and everyone ran in different directions, trying to find a place of safety. I went to the left as the others went right but I chose the wrong way.

The mortar bomb exploded just beside me and I could not remember a thing. I just blacked out and was left, for the men were too busy trying to save their own lives. I never knew it at the time but as I never turned up to be counted, my name was put down as a casualty, to be picked up later by the medics. What happened to the Germans in the opposite field I never did find out. Eventually I got to my feet but felt very weak and unsteady. Everything was quiet, nothing seemed to stir and I felt like I was in another world.

After some time, I started to remember things

and I could see more clearly. Raising myself, I pushed a piece of leafy bush away from my body and to my surprise I could stand upright. A piece of shrapnel was sticking out of my right leg but I was able to remove the piece and tie a bit of my shirt around the gash. Not long after this I was able to rejoin my squad of men and some of the soldiers had signs of tears on their dirty, stained faces for I do believe they all thought I was dead. It was not usual to see another man sobbing at a death but it shows how much a soldier's life meant to his comrades, for we were all like brothers.

The evening had turned into dusk as we found a place of refuge and we dug in for the night. The large, yellow moon was well into the star-studded sky and, as one of the men stood as sentry, the rest of us slid into our deep, dark foxholes to instantly fall into a deep sleep. The soldier on sentry duty could only have heard the sound of someone snoring and occasionally the odd yell of someone having a nightmare. The night passed peacefully and the following morning everyone was wide awake but dreading what the day would bring.

We had a drink from our canteens and were lucky enough to have the odd ration. It was always cold food from a tin or small package. The sergeant estimated we were about two miles from the front line and so deemed it quite safe for us to have a break and put our feet up for a while. So we had a rest and it did all the men a world of good, as we all were knackered. Then we had another stroke of luck. A runner came up from the rear to tell our officer that we were to wait in this large area for replacements and supplies to reach us. To be able to put our feet up for another spell was surely a surprise but to be told the platoon could stay even longer was a real bonus.

Sometime during the day, the new recruits turned up and I counted three dozen of them. They were around eighteen to twenty and all appeared frightened. Looking at them I realised that one day, before too long, they would also become old hands, if they lived long enough. But they would never stop being afraid!

Filling my helmet with water, I listened to the news the men had brought up from somewhere in the rear and some of it was very interesting. I washed my face as I listened, then stooped down a bit and bandaged the gash on my leg for it was trickling with blood. A lone medic, standing close, came over to me and re-examined my leg. 'OK, soldier,' he said, 'but if it gets any worse, report it,' and he walked off.

All day long we stopped in this place and it felt like paradise, but everyone knew that all good things must come to an end, so all canteens were filled with fresh water and we put as many rounds of cartridges in our belts as it was possible to carry. To our surprise, only half the platoon was moved forward – the other soldiers were told to remain where they were. This seemed very odd. The rest of us remained seated whilst the men vanished into the distance. God, it felt like a return to paradise. All day long we dwelt there, lying and sitting in groups, with enough time to have the odd nap.

We were to wait for orders to come to us, but we waited in vain and this was the only time I can ever remember us having such a long rest. By nightfall of the second day, we crawled back into the holes that were dug the previous night. This was another restless night for me. I gazed up at the bright stars and my thoughts were about the family I had left so long ago in America.

Finally, I dozed off with tears in my eyes, only to wake to the sound of voices, but feeling quite refreshed. The voice got louder and I heard someone yell, 'Shake a leg and let's have all you doughboys in line – this is another day of walking.' The platoon gathered around the sergeant to wait for further orders. 'We will today rejoin the rest of our command and with any luck this should not take long.'

A loud voice from behind shouted, 'Where are they?'

To my surprise the army officer replied, 'They are not very far away from Cherbourg.' For a minute he remained silent. 'That's all I can tell you at this moment so let's be on our way.'

At first the terrain was flat and very easy to walk on but then the rain came and it fell out of the sky in torrents. Before the soldiers knew it we were walking through water up to our ankles and we were soon dripping wet.

'Scout Nelson,' the sergeant said, 'go forward toward that hill and see if you can see the rest of our unit. If you do, signal back.'

Without hesitation, I turned to the left and found my way up through a wooded area. Finding a bunch of trees bent in all kinds of shapes, I looked closer and saw each one lying almost across each other in a criss-cross fashion with moss covering their bases. A young soldier wearing a Nazi uniform lay with wide open, sightless eyes, staring straight ahead. He had been dead for quite a while and had probably died during a bombing raid or the blitz of American artillery. I gazed with sadness as I noted that in the palm of his dirty, outstretched hand, he held a photograph of two small children and a pretty woman.

This was one of many times I felt distressed and bitter about this damn war. I gently closed his staring eyes and I'm not ashamed to admit I was sobbing as I slowly trudged from this scene. I climbed up a very high steep ridge and, as I came to the top, saw the rest of the company in the distance, so signalled the news to the sergeant and sat with my back against a tree to await them. Once back with my unit, I took my place in the long strung-out column to go forward, but always on the alert.

An hour later we were in action again. The sound of gunfire could be heard, just coming over the ridge. I was beckoned forward and went slightly ahead, leaving all the troops behind me. Finally, I arrived in an area that was field after field, all segregated by hedges and the occasional tree, but it was typical Normandy scenery. I clutched a piece of long turf from its side and hauled myself over it and fell flat on the other side. This turned out to be another unlucky day for me, for I fell into a very large pool of dirty water. I slid out of it saying under my breath a few nasty words, but not out loud and that probably saved my life.

I crouched down and slowly made my way backwards. I could just see one of my chums, out of the corner of my eye, going forward with the rest of the men in the next field and all seemed to be going well. I saw Peter Stobs, one of my best chums and waved my rifle at him and he waved in acknowledgment with a salute. I was still stooping over and literally crawling. I could not see what lay between the two small mounds on top of the hedge but heard the gun as it was fired and saw poor Peter fall to the soft, muddy ground. Looking up, I could see the bolt-action rifle still smoking and without even thinking reached up, grabbed the weapon and pulled it towards me. What happened next really did surprise me for I had pulled the sniper over to my side of the hedge. He fell to the soft ground just at my feet but we each had a rifle. I released his gun and he swung it at me but I was just a little bit quicker and I fired a shot first. I will always remember the look on his face as he fell to earth.

If I had not been quiet as I crawled backwards or stopped when I did, the bullet would have been mine instead of poor Peter's.

Then, glancing to my side, I noticed all the troops in the field opposite had stopped when they saw one of their men shot and lying on the wet ground. After I had shot the German sniper, I raced to the high hedge to the right of me and jumped it and, as tall as it was, I never touched the grassy, green top. To my surprise I landed in the middle of a group of my very own platoon. Everybody there was taken by surprise at my coming from nowhere. Suddenly, a stick grenade landed right in the middle of the men and blew up.

Bedlam broke loose as each soldier tried to find cover. Some of them were so taken by surprise that they just stood and stared, as if in shock. The stick grenade had left about seven of the men lying on the ground, which left almost half the soldiers not wounded, but shell-shocked. Those lying on the earth needed medical attention but before anyone could move an inch, another grenade was hurled over the hedge. Fortunately, it landed quite away from its target.

All the men knew where the hand grenades were coming from, so without further ado, about fifteen of our men just chucked their own hand grenades back and then there were screams of agony and pain, followed by silence. I felt something wet and sticky running down my dirty, unshaven face and thought I had been wounded, but, running my hands over it, gave a sigh of relief. It was only sweat.

The platoon never checked up to find if all the enemy had been eliminated for it was such a large area but I do know that the remainder of the men looked over the high hedge where the grenades were thrown and found three dead Germans who would not be throwing any more! The good old medics were soon on the scene and in total we had two dead and two more were out of action for the duration of the war. They were taken away on a stretcher.

When I was a boy, I never gave religion much thought, as I knew nothing about it. But during the odd days of fighting it became part of my life. There was never a day that I did not give a silent prayer and at the end of each long, daylight hour a quiet thank you to God, for helping me to survive.

Sometime later, in the mid-afternoon – this was just after the German stick-grenade episode – we were able to reach the opposite field. Finding nothing there, the platoon proceeded slowly to go forward again. Occasionally, the scouts up front would sight a large tank not too far in the distance but it was difficult to say whether it was one of ours or a German tank.

The digging of the slit trenches and foxholes became part of protecting ourselves and sometimes, if the ground was rocky or hard, you had to find another spot to dig in. On one occasion, when I was about two feet deep, I struck a water well and the damn water filled the foxhole in a matter of minutes. One very dark night, the company saw a village in the distance and the sergeant gave us orders to dig in and await the morning. One of the PFCs and I went to the edge of a green hedge and both of us took turns digging just below the bank. This left a small leafy tree shoot growing just above us.

Two hours later, the job was finished and, as

twilight turned to night, we crawled into it and leaned our M1 rifles against the side. The foxhole was dug very wide and deep, and both of us were well out of sight, but sitting down in it we were a bit cramped. A dark cloud shut out the glow of the moon and all at once thunder could be heard in the distance. To our dismay it started to pour with large drops of rain. Reaching above, we pulled and tugged the end of the small tree over the hole. This did seem to stop some of the raindrops from entering the hole but as time went by the big puddle at the bottom of our foxhole spread until we were sitting in water.

'Do you know what,' said my buddy, 'I think it's about time we made a move.' So the two of us climbed out of the watery hole to seek shelter somewhere under the overhang of a hedge.

I suppose in a way this was the bath we had not been able to take for a very long time. Mind you, I would have enjoyed a shave as well but it was not to be. I would think half the platoon was sheltering under the hedge but by the time the night ended everyone was soaked to the skin. The following day the whole platoon was on the move again.

As we marched, we saw a large field in the distance so the scouts were needed again. Four of us went a mile in front to keep our eyes open for any signs of an ambush.

I was somewhere around five hundred yards away from the other scouts and, as I went around a large wooded area, I came to an abrupt halt and looked into a field that stood on the outskirts of the trees and saw large, round poles sticking out upright from the ground. They were yards apart and, as there was no reason for them to be there, I went closer and saw the bodies of five young American soldiers spread-eagled on the wet ground, very near to a smashed-up glider.

The dead bodies must have been there since D-Day and the smell of death still lingered in the cool air. It made me feel so unwell. I just wanted to throw up! Stopping to look down at one of the bodies, I saw the face of a young man about my age. I remember thinking to myself, this could have been me lying here, for I was offered the chance of changing from infantry to become a para, many months before, but had turned it down. I just could not see myself jumping out of a plane and so I picked the lesser of two evils. This young soldier may not have had any choice and was probably conscripted for this regiment. Leaving this place of carnage, filled with sadness and a heavy heart, I knew the only consolation was that now, at least, after my report, they would be picked up for a decent burial.

Returning to my platoon took quite a long time as I had wandered a long way from them, and as I came near, they were close to a small forest. I looked just above the soldiers as they walked along with guns held ready. They were so interested in what was around them they did not notice the sniper sitting above them on a thick branch, looking at the soldiers passing below.

I aimed very quickly and fired a shot at him. Instead of hitting my target, it was the branch I hit, just beside him. He plummeted to the rain-soaked ground, landing just in front of a walking soldier. He was quickly taken prisoner but the amazing part of this capture came as I rejoined my platoon and found out that the man they had captured was in civilian clothing. I never did find out the outcome of this odd mystery. Shortly after the capture of this prisoner, he was taken away for interrogation.

I reported what I had seen and done, the captain uttered, 'Well done, Nelson, and also for helping in the capture of the sniper, now find your place to bed down for the night.'

'Yes, sir,' I replied and about-turned to dig my hole.

Digging In

The next morning, the platoon had not walked more than ten miles on the dusty road and through hedged fields, when in front of us could be seen a large town. It was difficult to tell how large it was but it was the biggest we had seen yet.

The entire company came to a halt just before reaching the outskirts and, before we could go on, Tiger tanks were seen moving quickly out of the town heading in our direction. Nearly half of the company had been issued with anti-tank grenades (an odd kind of shell, shaped like an oval rocket, but fired with a special bullet). Seven men formed a double line, loaded their rifles, took careful aim and fired, knocking the tread from many of the Tigers' wheels. Knowing they would be captured, the remaining tanks scurried away from the danger.

Whilst all this was happening, the foot soldiers had got even closer to the large group of people who were watching the tank fight from every window and doorway. To me, at that time, it seemed as if they could not care less if we had won. Having no tanks to contend with meant we could, and most certainly would, liberate this town from the Jerries. It did not take long before the entire platoon was just inside the town's boundary.

The town was very spread out but had many main streets, with rows of houses on both sides of the wide roads with the occasional shop separating them, reminiscent of a typical, old English village. Two of the squads of men waited on the end of the street nearest to us and three other squads began searching each house for any hidden enemy. This was a long, tedious job and lasted all day. Even then we were not finished.

We not only had to put up with the French antics, but also the damn Germans. It was difficult for us to tell a German from a Frenchman, for we only knew a few words of their language and could only go by their dress. We had captured or killed about a dozen men and lost two. The beautiful building in the square was a large grey-stone church and, at the sight of a bullet hole in the big leaded-glass window, I could not help stopping.

The large tower in front of the door was raising high into the air. What the other men did not see was a rifle resting on the ledge of the window, just hidden by a red-yellow stone jutting out of it. Acting on instinct, I just aimed and fired in one motion. The large window slammed shut as the force of the body hit it, and the enemy sniper plunged past the aperture and just landed beyond the soldiers. It was sheer luck I had seen him, for the burp gun (hand machine gun) also landed just in front of his body.

At long last, we had searched all the buildings and reluctantly allowed the people (most were holed up inside the great church), to return to their homes. Even then, we couldn't be sure that there were no Germans among the French civilians. We had no choice but to let them all go. We had searched about three quarters of the town and it had taken the company until the following afternoon. The captain was pleased at what had been accomplished, and as the last man left the town, the military police unit took command and would be left to finish the task.

The entire company then had permission to make our final camp for the night, just outside the town. I believe every soldier thought this was very unfair, but orders were orders, so about five sentries were put on special guard and the rest of the tired group dug their foxholes for the night. I was that damn tired I cannot even remember digging my hole and crawling into it. However, I do know I enjoyed a deep sleep but cannot recall how long I was asleep, for I awoke during the darkness to hear voices and activity just beyond my resting place.

Glancing out of my hole, I saw a line of German soldiers walking some distance away, who quickly vanished into the darkness. At sunrise the next morning, I reported what I had seen to the captain, and was told to forget it, but to keep my eyes peeled, as the Jerries could be waiting somewhere ahead. As I walked, my mind was not on the war, for I was thinking of Peter Stobs, the man shot by the German I had later killed. Peter was probably the best friend I'd made in my army days, but there were also others.

I started to recall my other buddies who had died. Sergeant Carter was one of the very first of my friends to be killed – he had his face literally blown to pieces – and Sergeant Bowchamp – the former cook – had died whilst cooking the big rooster. Privates Lazar, Cotton and Williams all perished. There were others – in fact, far too many to name, but who will for ever remain in my memory.

We can all make stupid mistakes at any time in our lives, but these can be fatal, especially during war, and one of the soldiers I knew very well made one that took his young life, even though he was told not to do it.

Each hand grenade has a ring above it and this in turn is attached to a pin. Once the pin is pulled, in five seconds the hand grenade will explode. The grenade was kept always in one's pocket.

Private Oliver was acting big. He attached three grenades to his belt, by their rings. I was well in front as we approached and jumped a hedgerow. All we heard was one big explosion. Dropping down to the ground, I looked to my left and there was not much left of Oliver. But his mistake also killed two of the soldiers just beside him. I often think of this incident, it taught me a lesson I will never forget – only put grenades in a tight-fitting pocket!

My feet were aching and I had a large sore on my left foot. God, I was tired, I had not eaten for God knows how long and my canteen was nearly empty, but I kept on walking. Sometimes, I felt like I had walked across the continent of Europe.

During my scouting in France, I learnt about racial prejudice. I was walking with another scout from the Deep South. The subject arose about coloured soldiers. He said that he couldn't mix with any black man and, as for fighting with him, he would rather die! He meant every word. I knew there was friction between the blacks and whites of the North and South but, even as he spoke, I knew there always would be, for the whites who lived there could not forget those people were once slaves.

I took my eyes off him for a moment to look at the smoke curling up in the distance but he carried on speaking, and he put it in very simple words and as he spoke I realised why the blacks and whites never mixed. And, of course, he was right, for the problem went back to the civil war when blacks were freed from slavery. A large number of southerners would never forgive or forget. So even up to the Second World War, they were kept well apart.

We had been walking all morning when, without any notice, the entire company was stopped and all our platoon sergeants were ushered forward to receive new orders. It seemed that the Germans, according to intelligence, were many miles in front of our position, so we were to await transport. As I recall, up until then, this had never happened before, but I think everyone was looking forward to the ride and it would give our poor feet a rest.

Later on, the long line of lorries did appear and drew up to where we were waiting. This was to be my second sighting of a black man. In fact, all the drivers of the transport were coloured. It appeared that the soldier I talked to was right when he said, 'The only place in the army that you will see a coloured man will be a non-combat unit – drivers and the like – because they could not be trusted to fight alongside Southern whites.' This was why I had never met a black man in front-line action. Remember, this all happened in the forties and, even today, a certain amount of hatred and mistrust still exists. However, this must not devalue the work that the black soldiers did since their actions during this horrible war did the American army proud!

All of us had a very uncomfortable ride in the canvas-backed lorry, for about an hour over bumpy roads and around large holes in the hard earth made by recent artillery shells. Then, of course, another bloomer occurred. The information we had received about the enemy, was totally wrong. Instead of the German line being in front, we were already in no-man's-land. Twelve lorries full of soldiers drove along a long, dusty road. There was plenty of space between each vehicle, and if this had not been so, then countless more lives would have been lost. I was sitting just behind the top sergeant, who was in turn sat behind the African-American driver and, therefore, I was looking between the two of them, out through the big, long windscreen. We travelled along a straight road and, approaching a large bend, went around it. I got a shock, for sitting facing us was a panzer tank.

The driver swerved the truck over the banking beside the road, just as the tank fired its first shell. We were already off the long road and running down a slight incline, so the shell never touched us, but the lorry behind was not so lucky. The shell struck it dead centre and, although I cannot be sure, I would bet not one of the soldiers survived that shell. The vehicles in the far rear were able to pull up on the side of the road and everyone tried to find a place of refuge.

The lorry I was in was certainly in dire trouble, for we were flung into the air, and as it came to rest, it slowly stopped on its top, leaving everyone lying in a heap. Considering the state of the vehicle and the way it landed, we were very lucky to have escaped without any casualties. Every one of the men, including me, suffered minor bruising, but no one died. I crawled out from under the rear of the big vehicle, being very careful not to touch the bent and sharp pieces of metal jutting out from the chassis. Everyone made their way up the grassy bank to rejoin the rest of the outfit, passing the blazing vehicle that was hit and the twelve bodies lying beside it.

With the roadway now empty of the panzer tanks,

we were able to place the dead bodies on another lorry to be dropped off sometime later. Then we all received the information we should have had before boarding the lorries. The Germans were closer than the captain realised and the platoon was nearly two miles inside the front line. Then a member of the top brass must have sensed the men could not return by transport, so the drivers were ordered to retreat back behind the line and we had no option but to walk forward and hope for the best.

Once again, the scouts were sent a distance in front of the platoon, to search the terrain in front and see if we could catch sight of the Germans. We saw signs of where the Tigers had gone. Then we saw a group of enemy soldiers, waving a white flag with their arms above their heads. Raising my rifle as they came nearer, I beckoned the one holding the flag to come closer. In a frightened voice I heard him say 'Comrade' and he started to talk to me in German. But I could not understand a word he said and so with my rifle pointing at their backs, I took them back to the platoon captain. The surprise on his face as I led them to him only lasted about a minute, then they were taken to the back of the front line for questioning and I resumed my scouting.

The countryside contained so many hills and valleys that it became almost impossible to tell if the Jerries were near, so three more scouts were sent to join in my search and that made four of us. On and on the platoon walked with a major who joined our company and he was slowly walking somewhere in the rear. The men were walking quite a distance apart, partly on the dirt road and everything could be seen. Not long after, we came to an old wooden signpost with three arrows pointing different ways but the one we took particular note of pointed the way we were travelling.

Passing the sign, we walked at least another half an hour and then, rounding some bushes and trees, we saw the outskirts of a large town.

Soon the soldiers from the platoon were all standing on a long hill and the captain had joined us. All around were men lying on the ground, with their machine guns and rifles pointed at the houses. Then the captain and sergeant spoke to each other and after a while a decision was made. They called all the platoon leaders together to give them their orders. We were told to walk toward the buildings, leaving plenty of space between each soldier and to take no extra risks. So very slowly the men walked, looking to the left and right as we went forward. Many of the people in this big town appeared at times on the fringe of the buildings but did not take much notice of us. As we got closer they seemed to vanish in seconds, leaving an empty area. The reason why became obvious very quickly.

All of the front-line men had entered the fringe of the city and before us was a dilapidated, old house. We all figured no one lived here since it looked vacant but in a way everyone felt uneasy

Bill's home in Camden, Maine

*Bill's family (top row, left to right) Ralph, Betty, Mum, Dad, Thelma
(Bottom row, left to right) Freda, Stella, Vincent, Bill*

Bill's wedding day on 25 February 1945

Bill's family reunion

Bill's sons (left to right) Terry, David, Paul

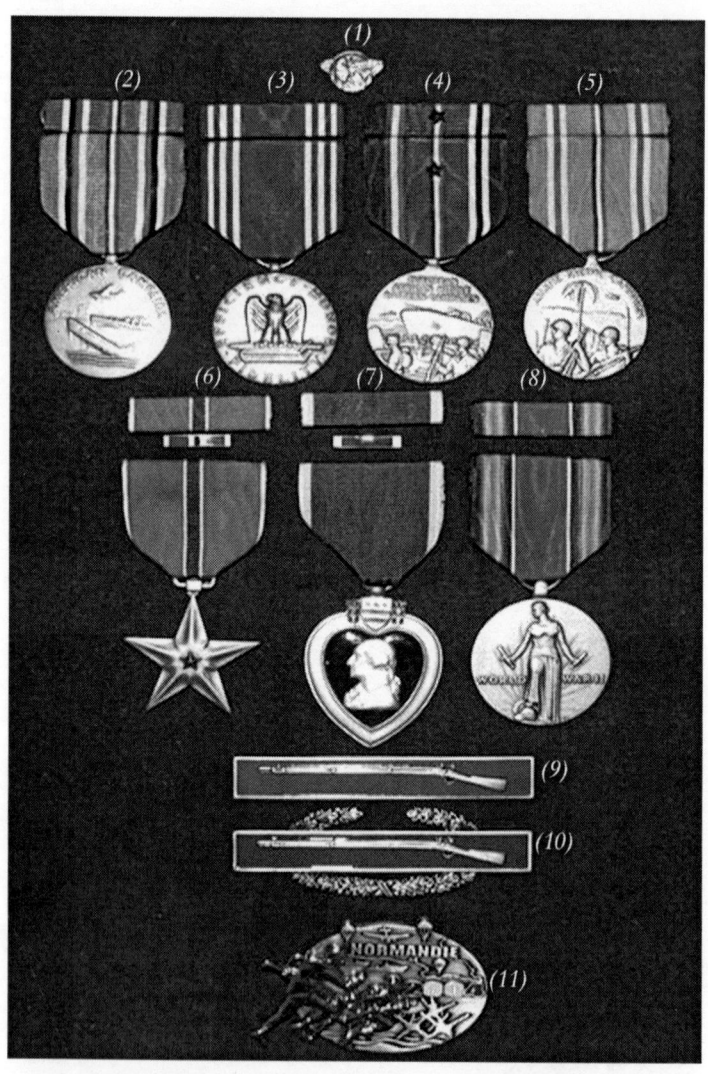

1 - *Honourable Service Lapel Button,* **2** - *American Campaign Medal,*
3 - *Good Conduct Medal,* **4** - *European-African-Middle Eastern Campaign Medal*
5 - *Asiatic Pacific Campaign Medal,* **6** - *Bronze Star Medal,* **7** - *Purple Heart Medal*
8 - *WWII Victory Medal,* **9** - *Expert Infantryman Badge,*
10 - *Combat Infantryman Badge,*
11 - *60th Anniversary D-Day Commemorative Chest Badge*

about this place, as if there was some evil involved and, as it happened, there was. The other men were just behind me, as I entered the road beside this old dwelling. Then I saw the danger and heard the shot as the German fired his gun. My guardian angel must have been hovering over me for, as the gun was fired, I dived just behind a garden fence that stood before me but I still had sense enough to fire my rifle at the tall shadowy figures of one of the Germans and God knows I counted at least five of them.

I landed on all fours, hitting the hard, brown earth, believing myself to be safe as long as I could stay under cover, but I knew I could not remain in this position for very long. Now I had to help eliminate the five Jerries firing at my soldier friends, who seemed to be well hidden but still vulnerable.

From my hiding place I saw the first of the five Germans. He was in plain sight. He never knew what hit him, as the bullet struck and he fell to the wet ground. The others were very well protected because they were shooting from an old shed. The rickety door was hanging on its hinges, which made my task easier, for I took the hand grenade from my pocket, pulled the pin and hurled it at the partially open door. I counted to four as I lay flat on the ground and on the fifth count it blew up.

Getting to my feet, I looked between parts of the wood-framed gate. With sheer luck it must have hit the side of the door and rolled inside. As I looked, some of this large shed was smoking – a slight flame was coming from the hole where the door had been. I felt I had done my share of the fighting that day. At long last, the platoon was able to go inside the boundaries. All around soldiers were dead or wounded. Many of our men had entered the large town's outskirts. It was now safe for them to take up their posts inside it. The Germans, in the meantime, must have dispersed or hidden further back in the town but the Americans were very close behind them.

So began the task of liberating the town, which we knew would take a very long time. We all knew that, without doing this, we would never feel safe. This was the largest place we had so far encountered. It took more men to search and liberate and so the entire company was ordered to give a helping hand.

The sergeant walked quickly to the side of the street yelling, 'I want every person who lives in these homes to come out of hiding and stand in the middle of the street. Every property will be searched.' He paused, then spoke again. 'If anyone disobeys this order they will be taken prisoner and could be shot.'

He then walked back and gave the order that there were to be five men in each group who were to search on each side of every street. This took all the men in the company, for there were many streets and houses to be made safe. Many of them had to be finished by nightfall. One thing in our favour was that it stayed light until quite late.

The liberation of Saint-Lô went beyond all expectations, for the inhabitants of the large town acted with a speed that amazed everyone. They gathered in large numbers in the middle of the roadway, each of them jabbering in French, as the men inspected the houses in each street. Occasionally, a shot was heard but, as time went by, it became very quiet. Many groups of men were searching the houses. I think the five in my group searched for miles, or so it seemed.

We came upon a large grey-stoned church and, as we viewed it, a shot was heard. One of the men fell in front of me. As the rifle shot was heard, I flung myself quickly to the ground, just below a gravestone. The other three did likewise. Three German soldiers stood just in front of the church door, with hands above their heads. The fourth German stood quite a distance away, with smoke coming from his gun. He had already pointed his rifle at me and, to my amazement, as he pulled the trigger the weapon clicked – he had a dead shell in the cylinder! I knew I was a very lucky man and was glad I had not suffered the fate of my friends. The German was also lucky, for he threw his hands in the air, dropping his rifle in the process. We nearly shot him. Indeed, we wanted to, but we could never shoot an unarmed man.

At dusk the following day, the officer was satisfied that the town had been liberated. We all gave a sigh of relief.

As our infantry platoon went out of the town, I knew that we would not be allowed to return. The military police were already on the scene and it became their responsibility, as always, to patrol the town and generally keep the peace.

After leaving the outskirts of the built-up area, the platoon had to find a place to rest, as it was becoming dark. We all gathered in a large grassy field just outside Saint-Lô. It had a road running just beside a tall tree-stumped hedge, with a big arrow pointing up the dusty street bearing the name 'Cherbourg'.

Looking to our right, I saw trees on the horizon. Gradually the darkness closed in. As the huge yellow moon rose, we also, to our surprise, saw ripples on water. As the moon showed through the clouds, its rays revealed a river just beyond the town. My buddy just beside me remarked, 'What a still night this is!' and, as we watched, a tracer bullet was seen rising in the sky like a shooting star. Shortly afterwards, whilst sitting in my foxhole, I fell into a deep sleep.

At first light, the platoon was on its way again, walking in a long, crooked, strung-out line ever alert, searching the area as we went. We then approached a long, winding river where the water was flowing very fast. Getting closer to it, we found that the bridge that had at one time spanned the river had been blown up and was lying crumbled in the wet mud beside some bushes. Most of the platoon had stopped beside this river, wondering how the hell we would get across.

The soldier just beside me saw a mirror-like

flash at the same time I did and both of us flung ourselves to the earth. At the first sound of gunfire, all hell broke loose. The men who had arrived at the river first had run into a very well planned ambush. Then, above the sound of gunfire, the yelling and shouting for help could be heard. We were in no position to give it! Everyone not already dead or wounded was shooting at anything that moved across the water.

Sergeant Young, one of those who had landed on Omaha Beach, had become one of the first victims to die and lay just beside me, with outstretched hands pointing at the water. But other than feeling sad, there was literally nothing I, or anyone else, could do.

The ruse the Germans used was plain to see, they had regrouped after crossing the bridge, destroyed it, knowing we would sooner or later turn up and laid a well-planned ambush. Part of the platoon was in trouble and every other man was pinned to the earth and could not go forward or back. Only occasionally did we see something across the water to shoot at. Many men died that day, and many more surely would have, but somehow, our luck changed, for the artillery had been called to help us. This took time, so whilst we waited we had to lie on very dark, smelly earth and more or less pray to God that we would survive.

Before the .155 artillery shells came into action, two large Sherman tanks had arrived on the scene, blasting shells across the fast, glistening waters, and all at once the noise from the rifles and burp guns went silent, and in their place was heard the sound of the big heavy guns and then more shells from the tanks.

'God, Buddy,' said an unkempt soldier, 'I would say we were as near to hell as we will ever get. What do you say?'

I looked at him. 'My friend, we are in hell!'

Then the noise and fighting at last ceased but we all remained where we were for quite a long time, then all of us walked slowly back and away from the river to leave the medics to tend to the dead and wounded.

'Come on, you lot!' yelled an irate sergeant, 'spread out and follow me. Let's follow along this damn river until we find a safe place to cross.'

What we had been looking for came into sight. Just around a clump of bushes and beside a huge boulder was a rickety old wooden bridge but only the foundation was left. We were able to go across, even though we all got soaking wet. But then, I bet everyone needed a bath. At long last, we made the other side and waited for the sergeant to give his orders. He pointed his finger at me.

'See those trees just beyond that river, Nelson? Well, I want you and Andrews to search the vicinity of that area' he pointed 'just in front of those trees and across the river was where the ambush had taken place, so take extreme care, in case the damn Germans are still about.'

Thus Andrews and I left the platoon and, walking a long way in front, slowly made our way towards the far-off treeline.

Around seven o'clock, we approached a small wooded area. A dark mist was hanging over the tall trees, making it difficult to see anything along the hazy edge. Four or five hundred yards before the line, a bushy terrain appeared, and as the two of us began to approach a large clump of bushes, a shot was heard. Looking to my right, I saw Private Andrew spread-eagled on the ground with his gun tightly clutched in his left hand.

Throwing myself to the left, I fell beside a bush and could almost feel the bullet as it passed my head. I knew if I moved an inch I would be a dead man and so there was just one alternative... play dead. My eyes were slightly open and I was able to see nearly everything in front of me. A long time later, a very tall German appeared. He walked over to Andrews, prodded him with his foot and kicked him so hard he rolled over on his back. Then he just looked into his face and prodded him again to see if he was alive. He looked satisfied and then walked over to me.

The German had just drawn his long booted leg back to give me a thump when he realised I was only play acting. He slung his rifle very quickly up but he was too slow and he fell just by my side as I shot him in the upper part of his leg, dropping his gun as he did so. I can still see the look of disbelief as he stared at the gun inches from his helmet. Then, out of the trees, three other Germans came running and I could see that one of them was wearing civilian clothing. Two of them had rifles, the third was holding a revolver, but all three of them came to a stop when they saw where my rifle was pointing. I'm sure they thought I was easy prey. Keeping my rifle pointed and my finger on the trigger, I raised my other hand and made a slicing motion at the German's neck. Their reaction was instantaneous, for they all shouted, 'Nein, nein, nein!' though at that time I never knew what this meant until later. They were obviously very frightened and surrendered immediately. My gamble had paid off.

Walking back over to Andrews, I found to my utter delight and surprise that he was alive but unconscious and so no time could be wasted. Two of the prisoners carried Andrews and the other one, who was dressed as a civilian, aided the other wounded German. Not long after, as luck would have it, we saw the platoon slowly coming towards us. I know everyone was surprised to see a scout coming back from a scouting order with four prisoners in tow. When they saw Andrews, a medic was quickly called and he was taken back behind the front line. Then I reported to the officer in charge and told him what had taken place and how the Germans were taken prisoner. He congratulated me and told me to rest. We were all digging our foxholes, for dusk was closing in, but just as we were digging, a noise was heard. A group of young soldiers appeared and these were the replacements to make up for the many men we had lost on the previous day. I lay in my hole and soon fell asleep.

It seemed but minutes before dawn arrived and

everyone began crawling out of their foxholes. 'Now then, today,' said the sergeant, 'we will make for the other group of trees seen away to our left.'

He turned towards me and said, 'You, Corporal Nelson, I would like you and Private Jones to be the scouts needed, so let's be having the two of you.'

Jones and I hurried away to the left of the company and, again, went a long way forward. The green-leafed trees soon appeared but it was not a very large glade, only a few trees, but they were very closely packed together. Jones pointed to me, he was just going around the trees and I went around the other way.

We would meet up on the other side but, just as I was going around the greenery, about 400 yards away there was the sound of the fluttering of blackbirds. They flew out of the woods, making me stop to stare at the many mounds of earth piled high just outside the big trees. I knew full well that if anyone was hiding, I would be a dead soldier by now and so I slowly approached and looked into a wide, deep trench.

Even today, I cannot understand what had happened at this odd place, for I saw many bodies lying on their backs. They all wore civilian clothes. Nearby was another trench. In that, I saw the bodies of women. It was a sickening sight!

I went further around the woods and was deep in thought, but I was just not concentrating on my job. The first mortar shell fell just to my right, blowing a very large hole in the ground. I fell to earth, rolling over a mound of mossy dirt, but knew the mortar crew had chosen me as their target and so the second shell would be even closer. I got up to run like hell towards the leafy trees but only got within fifty yards when I was blown off my feet and fell to the ground.

Many times I have deemed myself lucky and again it happened for, instead of being killed, I was only slightly wounded. I could feel the blood running down my leg and I had been struck by a piece of shrapnel. Every soldier carries some type of bandage, so as I lay in the hole, I tied this around my leg to stop the bleeding. The platoon arrived soon afterwards but there was no sign of the German mortar crew. The medics put a new bandage on my leg and again I dug a deep foxhole for the coming night.

The last few nights I'd had wicked nightmares – the same dream kept recurring. I was always stepping over dead bodies, all their heads were looking up at me and I saw the faces glaring and smiling. The faces were always the same, for they always bore the features of the man I'd shot at the hedgerow. I was even walking in my sleep and many times was led back to my foxhole by one of my chums.

However, getting up the following morning, I found that I had slept the night without having my usual nightmares. I felt quite refreshed but it had been raining and so I was uncomfortably wet! It was a damp, misty day and, as I looked towards the sky, I could see the sun trying to break through. Everyone got up and assembled for their orders. It appeared that soldiers of the engineering corps had failed to capture a stronghold further forward and had to retreat, so our platoon was asked to do the job, ever mindful, of course, to be alert and adopt the correct walking distance throughout. All day we walked and to the platoon leaders' surprise, the men found hardly any resistance. What we did occasionally see were many dead bodies of bloated, partly eaten animals.

Coming to a large field, I saw a herd of cows grazing and thought what a brilliant idea it would be to fill my canteen with fresh milk. I then approached one of the cows very cautiously. But there was no need for such caution, she just stood very still as I drew near. Sitting on the wet ground beneath the cow, I took my tin canteen cup in my left hand, my right hand pulled the teats but much to my surprise and horror, the tin cup was nearly filled to the top with a dark green substance, nothing like what I had expected.

These animals had not been milked for quite a few days. I stayed where I was and milked the poor beast dry and in the end probably saved her life. I knew it was really a very foolish thing for me to do, loitering too long in one place, but when I arose to walk away I felt very proud of myself.

There seemed to be no respite, only walking ahead, looking for signs of the German army.

Later in the afternoon, we passed through the large courtyard of a thatched farmhouse. Everywhere seemed devoid of life, but when we passed the old building, I noticed the curtains were pulled apart and I had a premonition that the whole platoon was being kept under strict surveillance. The lead man opened the ancient gate at the end of the yard and we all fanned out, going away from the farm, then we trudged up the slight slope that led into a dust-covered road. I looked back and was not surprised to see three children come out of the house to gaze at us. Why could they have not invited us with open arms instead of all this secrecy? In a way it made me wonder whether the French wanted to be liberated, or was this even a French family?

Then another building came into view. All of the inhabitants were at the gate shouting at us in French and passed us lots of drinks as we went by. This was a tonic to the tired men. We walked for a couple of hours before the afternoon became dusk. The whole company split up and each platoon dropped out, one by one, to dig in for the night.

My platoon was the last to find a place for the night. There was no moon, only the dull, hazy clouds drifting in the night sky. We could just make out the hedgerows that surrounded our whole platoon and could see the tall, huge hill towering upwards from the next field and so we were planning to dig in just below. We were completely unaware of any danger but then we were so tired that we hardly took notice of anything.

We entered the hedged field but found we were not alone, for there were about a dozen brown cows sharing the area with us. I was damn pleased there was no bull with them! In the darkness, I made out a very large tree in the middle of the field and saw another with leafed branches waving in the night air. The orders had been to fall out, dig in and post sentries. Each soldier wandered off to seek a quiet, suitable place to dig a foxhole. It was really dark by then, but once in a while the large, yellow moon did show its face through the misty sky and brighten up the earth.

Little did we know that the place we were digging in was a waiting death trap. The Germans knew we were in the field from the moment we walked into it. Between the shafts of moonlight they would have seen us and when it was very dark they were certain to have heard the sounds of digging going on in the meadow, so all they had to do was simply wait for daylight.

Like the rest of the large platoon, I never even gave this a second thought, for being so dirty and tired, I said to myself, 'To hell with everything.'

I found myself a place behind the tall hedge facing the hill, I laid my rifle beside me and fell into a deep sleep, whilst the rest of the men were digging their foxholes.

What awoke me was a loud thud on the other side of the hedge. Before I could even look over it, an .88 artillery shell exploded very close to me. Soldiers who had taken one or two hours to dig their holes were literally blown out of them. The holes, deep as they were, did not prevent the shells from hitting the side of the hedge and exploding in the holes. God, whoever thought this was a safe area to spend the night probably never had brains. As if this was not enough, the mortar shells were landing in the field and burp guns were now active. The sound of mortally wounded men screaming out in pain and agony could be heard above the shelling and the noise from the burp guns. One of the large trees was blown apart and the other had the dead remains of a cow hanging from its branches, which added to the collective slaughter. Before my eyes, I saw another cow go up and over me, to be blown apart. Only a few of the unfortunate animals remained in one piece in this hedged field.

Without question, the gunner knew his business, for mortar and artillery shells were exploding all around our hiding places. Then the remainder of those poor cows were seen to be floating in the air and, where they once stood, I could only see pools of bright blood. I raised my head, looked at the dark sky and closed my eyes as I said a few words of prayer but, as I did so, flecks of blood were landing on my face. Brushing my hand across my wet face, I looked around at all the destruction. I again gave thanks, for if I had not been too damn tired to dig a hole the previous night, by now I'd probably be like those poor cows.

I was just behind the big hedge facing the Jerries and so they could not see me. I very slowly crept backwards, staying close to the hedge. Not too far away, I saw the exit gate. Crossing my fingers, I stood up and made a dash for it. To this day, I don't know how I survived, for it seemed that every one of the Germans was firing at me. The nearest they got was when a lump of shrapnel tore a bit of skin from my left leg and this was just before I jumped over the gate.

I would have stopped to fight but how the hell can one kill shadows? So with a lot of my chums, I raced past a bush thicket and as I did so, I saw a good friend of mine lying on his side with a cloth tourniquet around the top of his left thigh. The flow of blood had stopped but he still needed treatment for his wound. I slung my rifle over my shoulder, stooped down, picked him up but then nearly dropped him because he was so heavy. I carried him away from the battlefield and could not help anyone else and God knows there were plenty of others needing help that day. I was told my act of heroism would be reported. This meant nothing to me but then, I remember thinking, at least this soldier chum was alive and would be taken out of this wicked war. I thought all this as I placed him at the feet of a medic.

I never expected any reward for what I had done, for I believe many a soldier would have done the same, but the army did make me feel as if I had achieved something special. Many good men died that days and they will always be in my memory. When I hear the old poem of 'Flanders Fields', I will always think of my great comrades.

We got a certain amount of revenge on the enemy for killing so many of our young soldiers in the field, for a counterattack took place.

First, the artillery barrage kept on and on and, while this was on going, we attacked the Germans on the hill with every weapon available to us. I reckon we were two to one against them. Then, out of the blue, a Lockheed Lightning aeroplane came from nowhere to strafe the hill with machine gun fire. I'll bet the Germans thought all the American army was taking part but the shelling from above was getting less and less intense.

I returned to the field I had left and saw the remains of human bodies and animals scattered everywhere. Then, soldiers from another platoon and all of those who had survived in mine started to go up the hill. Every soldier who had taken part understood why we had lost so many of our comrades, for the hill was armed like a fortress with weapons of all types and all of them had been trained on the field below. As we went slowly up we saw many men lying dead from our own artillery fire. This battle was not yet won for near the top of this big, battle-scarred hill was a huge pillar block (mortar nest). It arose like a massive, cement dome from the wet earth.

I lay just behind a massive brown-gray boulder as all my chums went a bit closer and what happened next came as a complete surprise. I was watching a man as he got nearer, then he got up to run to another place for an extra bit of concealment but he never made it. There was a loud explosion and, I swear, he just seemed to disappear. He had run over a landmine and was blown to pieces.

The whole day from the start had been nothing but trouble and now this had happened. I was not only dirty, tired, and hungry but also scared and I began to wonder whether this was real life and why the hell was I there anyway. I got to my feet and ran towards another one of my chums.

I jumped over a middle-sized hedge gate, with my rifle held above my head, and as I jumped, felt a bullet enter my right wrist. My rifle dropped from my grasp as I fell to earth, with blood gushing from the wound. I do not believe I've ever been in such dreadful pain and I cried like a baby. Lying near a fence I clutched my wrist just above the wound to stop the flow of blood. As I arose from the dark earth, I could hear all my buddies and one stopped to bend over and helped me. He put a makeshift bandage on my wrist and this seemed to stop the blood flow and just a trickle came from underneath the cloth, but this did not relieve me of the severe pain. I learned later that the bullet had broken one of the bones running from the wrist to the elbow. It was not a clean break but rather it shattered the bone. I did not realise at the time but I was a very lucky man for it could have hit my head.

My leg had been playing me up, now it was my wrist, so what the hell could or would happen next? I somehow managed to hobble out of no man's land and, as I came towards the back line, was seen by a medic, who escorted me to a small, surgical tent. I was at the end of my tether; the strain and stress of war was telling on me.

The bullet had not only broken the arm bone but left splinters as it had passed through my wrist. An army doctor checked me over. I was in so much pain, they gave me an injection and I passed out. I remained in this medical tent all day and it was surprising to see the amount of wounded soldiers coming into the tent for treatment and also the amount of bodies that were being taken away.

Bearing in mind that penicillin was used for the first time (without any trials) during the Second World War, it turned out to be a gamble that really paid off. It became known as the wonder drug of that time and I had many more injections. Later on that evening, with my whole right arm in a rigid cast, I was escorted with a lot of other men to lorries and driven back, to see once again the blue waters of the Channel, with many large ships moored offshore. Although this was well up the coast and nowhere near Omaha Beach, it made me shake with mixed emotions. It seemed like the past had caught up with me and I believe I wept again.

I cannot remember very much of walking up the dry path to reach the small, wooden wharf but as I stepped upon it, I felt a hand upon my shoulder and a voice saying, 'Is that you, Buddy?' I looked at the man who spoke to me, realising instantly that it was a man born and bred in the town I came from and went to school with. He wore the blue of the navy and was serving in Europe. He held my hand

and chatted to me all the way across the Channel, but alas, we had to part at Folkestone. He waved goodbye to me as I went ashore and his ship left to return to France. I never got to see him again for he perished. I learnt this some months after my discharge.

I became a passenger in the back of an army lorry and we arrived later at a huge US army hospital situated in the Malvern Hills. I was checked in with seven other wounded soldiers. We were allocated a bunk each and, as it was nearly dark, we went to sleep. But I was still having those dreadful nightmares.

Wounding, Marriage and the Postal Unit in Japan

My stay at Malvern Hospital was just wonderful and I had nearly everything I desired. I sometimes thought it was like staying in a first-class hotel for it was like going to heaven to reside after staying in hell. This was how I felt at times, and so settling in was quite easy, but I was handicapped with having one arm (my right, being in a cast). They drugged me every night, for I continued to walk in my sleep. The treatment helped and soon the nightmares became less frequent. The US army hospital was a wonderful place to be and the army nurses and doctors were really nice.

I could not shave or write letters and found it very difficult to dress myself, but I did look forward to be being allowed to go into the town of Malvern Hills. Such a lovely place, in fact, it looked so much like the town I came from with its hills and scenery that it felt like the home I loved. Everything was going quite well and I had been in hospital a whole month when I had a set back. The day went very well, I arose in the morning, the nurse helped me to dress, wash and shave, then towards the evening I saw a few casualties arriving back from the front but never consciously gave it a thought.

When I went to bed that night, I had a very bad dream of my past and to this day can still remember it. In it, Private Jones and I were going through a hedged field and, about halfway across, there was one almighty explosion. The field was land-mined and poor Jones had stepped on one. He was flung into the air like a rag doll and never did know anything about it, for he died instantly. I felt myself stopping to stare in amazement, then ran like hell forwards and was lucky because I saw a hedgerow just in front and jumped over it. In my nightmare I could see the German staring at me as I landed in front of him, the look in his eyes as he was shot and his screaming woke me up from this dreadful dream.

Apart from the nightmares, the time I spent in this hospital really helped me a lot but, at last, the cast on my right arm was removed and I was declared fit to be transferred to an army rest home. In a way I was sorry to have left the hospital as the staff there were really wonderful. They would do nearly anything for their patients. They put me on an army lorry, shook my hand and sent me on my way to a lovely, restful camp in West Warwick, Leamington Spa, where I was to live out another part of my life in the army.

I soon settled again into the routine of army discipline and made many friends, some with combat memories and it kept me in touch with what was happening in the war zone. Again we were treated with the utmost respect by the heads of the camp. Many of them must have had front-line experience and known what the men had been asked to do. I met one soldier from another platoon and we became really good chums. We went out together for the odd drink of English bitter, visited a few local towns and were relaxed and cheerful.

The two of us men were invited to a 'wounded soldiers' get-together, a kind of party, comprising cups of tea and a chat to the young ladies present. This was to be the turning point of my whole life. Though I was twenty at the time, I never had time to fraternise or even to meet a young woman. Now I was about to fall head over heels in love with the most beautiful girl I had ever met. Her name was Joyce Bourner. There was a hitch, however – Joyce was from the city of London in England and I was a country bumpkin from the United States of America.

We first met at the Spa Hotel in Leamington and a Mrs Jenner introduced us to each other. And so began a love match that was never to be broken.

I went to London, where I met her widowed mother, Maud Bourner and we got on very well. Whilst we were in London, two or three doodlebugs (flying rockets) dropped out of the sky and I was told later, that one went down a bomb shelter, killing everyone in it.

Joyce and I had some wonderful times whilst I was in this camp. We met almost every night after she left work and went out together to different places. I believe it was termed a whirlwind courtship, for I soon proposed to her and to my delight she accepted.

I must admit that not all Yankees were as honest. I knew Yanks who lied and were already married back home and who boasted of having oil wells when they didn't have a penny. I'm not making out like I was a saint, but I meant every word I said to her. Joyce knew, though, to put it bluntly, that I had not got a 'pot to pee in' but we still accepted each other, even though I was a rash, country lad and she was a city girl. Joyce and I then had other things to talk over for, although I had just asked her to marry me, I had to get the US army's consent and it had to come from the chaplain. He had an interview with my wife-to-be and nearly all of the time was taken up with a discussion on our social and cultural differences.

One hour later, after talking to Joyce, the chaplain called for me to come into his room and we both sat down before him. After the chat, he gave us both his blessing. There was one small snag, however. I was twenty years old and would have had to get both my parents' permission. But as I only had one month to go before reaching twenty-one, we decided to wait to be wed and set the date for 25 February 1945.

Waiting proved to be very tiresome, for it seemed to be the same old routine every day. Kitchen police and sentry duty, as well as inspection, for it was wartime and so we were still on the alert. To make matters worse, I still could be sent back to the front before my marriage. I never told my wife-to-be this, as I didn't want to upset her.

Occasionally the past returned, but as time passed by, my mind turned to other things. This, I suppose, was due to my future wife's ability to make one forget and start living again. As usual, not everything went smoothly. Firstly, all of the papers regarding my marriage from the army's archives got mislaid, and secondly, I was being transferred to Sutton Coldfield near Birmingham. I immediately reapplied to the chaplain for consent to be reaffirmed.

In the meantime, I was sent to join a unit at my new camp. It seemed that I was totally fit, not for active service, but capable of doing a different job, so back to the army training I went, only this time, I had to learn about the postal service. No more lying about, kicking my feet. But this did not mean I had abandoned my wife-to-be, because on my days off I simply went to Birmingham by Number Two tram, then got on a train to Warwick to meet her.

I was put on many a charge because I was often late for roll call but I did not care. Then, out of the blue, came the good news that my wedding papers had finally been found, so the US army, after looking into my background, gave their consent so we could get married after my birthday.

I went to a theatre and saw a film featuring Charlie Chaplin and was laughing when the man sitting beside me began moaning in pain. He took his hands away from his face and, to my amazement, part of his face and both his hands were covered with small and large warts, mostly inflamed. I asked his name and he answered, 'I am Sergeant Carter.' To tell the truth, I felt very sorry for him. The way he looked, he probably would be shunned. To this day I will never know why I did it, but I took a copper cent and rubbed it over parts of his face and hands. I certainly would not say I believed it would make any difference but I asked him to pray for the warts to disappear as I rubbed them. Funny as it seemed, the coin I rubbed with became very cold. Then I tossed the copper coin down amongst our feet.

The funny film ended and, on my honour, two weeks later, I met Sergeant Carter again and lo and behold, he showed me both of his hands and pointed at his face and there were no signs of any warts. I know this is very hard to believe but I had never met this soldier before and if he reads this, he could and would vouch for everything I've said.

In no time, it was my twenty-first birthday and Joyce and I agreed that it really was a good time to be wed. We could not make it any sooner because by law, to be married in a church, the couple had to give twenty-one days' notice so that the marriage could be contested at the ceremony, to help prevent the crime of bigamy.

I asked a friend of mine in the unit to be my best man and his name was Private Musolf and together we got leave to travel to London by a fast-line Pullman train.

Joyce stopped with her mother, whilst my best man and I went to a place called Forest Hill, to stay for the night with her sister Mabel and husband Chester Reed. This was the first time I had met this part of her family. The day before the marriage, we saw some of the bombing London had gone through. Flats and houses were blown apart and sometimes whole estates were turned into dirty rubble. I remember at the time thinking, why civilians?

Then our big day arrived. All the people were waiting inside the large stone church, mostly my Joyce's family. As my mate Musolf and I walked down the aisle, everybody seemed to look very serene and happy. The best man and I took a seat and just in front of us, standing, was the minister, with a very large Bible resting in his hands. A few minutes later the Wedding March played and Joyce walked down to stand at my side and both of us faced the priest. The ceremony went as planned but in peacetime it probably would have taken a bit longer.

We said our vows, a prayer was spoken and about a half-hour later, we were pronounced man and wife and kissing her was like kissing an angel. The final task was to sign the register. There was no time for parties, for this was still wartime. The wedding photographs were taken, congratulations received and my wife and I went on a two-night honeymoon. Within the hour, the two of us had boarded a train to arrive in Birmingham sometime in the evening.

My wife worked as a shorthand typist in the Ministry of Defence and, like myself, could not expect a long honeymoon. Thus two nights in a Birmingham hotel were all they allowed us. What a time it turned out to be, doors were slamming all night and people were arguing in the next room. I'm sure if we had not had a chair against the door someone would have come in. Oh well, so much for a wartime honeymoon! I was happy and contented with what I had done, for now I was the husband of a lovely English bride.

After the honeymoon, my wife returned to her secretarial job and I journeyed forty miles away to Sutton Coldfield, and again joined my unit, to go back to being a soldier.

Whilst at the postal unit, I went for an interview with a panel of the top brass. This was quite an informal affair, no regimental discipline but just a test of my ability as a soldier. An army doctor was also in the same room. I was given many tests and at the end of it I was pronounced not active enough in my right hand to handle a rifle as it needed to be used in combat.

This was quite a shock to me, for physically, in all other ways, I passed fit, but the gunshot wound I had in my right wrist had left me with three dead fingers and the stress of the Omaha beach landing was also taken into account. This left the army with two options… to send me home to be discharged, or to put me for the remainder of the war in a non-combat regiment. As I did not want to leave the forces, they decided to put me into a postal unit, where at least my skill as a front-line soldier would come in, if needed. Later on, the major told me why the rifle was so important. Being a non-fighting unit, there was no reason to have weapons but the top brass thought they might be needed for protecting other soldiers' lives.

When I asked the young Englishwoman to marry me, I had no idea I was to be sent away so soon after our wedding, especially as I had just been informed she was carrying my first child. I had no say in this matter, as a soldier in the army I had to do as ordered. Although I would do as commanded, I thought it to be very unjust, for I had made and survived the D-Day landing on Omaha Beach and had been in many bloody battles for twenty-eight days before being wounded and now it seemed as a 'reward' I was to be shipped to another war zone but God knows where. I just had no option but to phone my young wife and tell her the bad news.

Officially, I was to leave England the following day, to an unknown destination. My wife was still crying as I told her I loved her very much and that she would always be in my thoughts. I also promised to send a letter as soon as I had reached my destination. As I replaced the telephone, I realised how my wife felt, not only would we miss each other, but she would also be carrying our baby without the two of us being together. I lay on my bunk that night, staring at the grey ceiling of the big Nissan hut and watched a small spider spinning a web. I thought to myself, maybe this little creature was a sign of good luck and everything would turn out to be OK.

That night turned out to be one of the longest I had ever spent, because I was tossing and turning in frustration. As the early dawn light shone through the window, a voice was shouting in my ear, 'Rise and shine, you doughboy.' And looking up with half-open eyes, I saw the sergeant pointing towards the far washroom and in a gruff, old voice he said, 'After everyone has finished in the latrines, get ready for transport. It will arrive after breakfast and we will be on our way.' But he still never mentioned where we were bound for.

He didn't tell us for, if he had, I just might have gone absent-without-leave and stopped with my wife. Instead, I lined up to climb aboard one of the lorries. There were about a hundred of us in total and we travelled many miles that day, until arriving at a port just as night time darkened the sky. The closing in of darkness made it impossible to name the port the big lorries drove into.

We knew it just had to be somewhere along the English Channel. Climbing down from our transport, we walked up a long, narrow gangplank and on to the deck of a large craft and I could just make out the word 'ferry' but owing to the light, I could not read anything else. Nearly an hour later, all the young soldiers had boarded and we were standing and sitting where we could find room. Suddenly, a loud voice shouted, 'Everyone will stand where they are and a roll call will be conducted by the sergeant.'

The sergeant took out a piece of paper and started to call out each name. When he was satisfied that all were present, he put it away saying, 'All of you can take it easy for now, but be ready to vacate the ship when we reach the other side.'

The huge, yellow moon was very high in the sky as the ship slowly crept into the harbour to stop at the dock. The gangplank was quickly lowered to the land of France. As I went down the gangplank to step on the earth it felt like a dream. Visions of blood and death were in my brain and it took a few seconds to realise this was all in the past. Where we landed I'll never know, but lorries were waiting just outside.

Each soldier was directed to a particular vehicle and climbed aboard. I can recall the driver of the canvas-topped lorry I was on, for he was grinning at me, then shook a finger at me. 'Shake a leg and climb aboard,' he said.

I could only just make out his features for his face was as black as night. As the lorries were filled with men, they formed a convoy and were driven away. The large vehicles were to be at least ten lengths apart and not travel faster than thirty miles an hour. Nearly every soldier sitting down, in a cramped position, fell asleep. There were sounds of snoring, coming from every truck and this went on until all of our transport arrived at the gates of Paris, the capital of France. I was sitting at the rear of the vehicle and thus was able to see the huge area we had gone through. I was surprised to observe nothing blown up or damaged and there were no signs of artillery or fighting anywhere.

I cannot remember where my regiment went after I was wounded but one thing I do know was that it would be very unlikely to leave a place as large as this city without the scars of the war. The transport crawled to a halt just outside a building and one by one each soldier climbed out of his vehicle and made his way to the large half-open door. Standing just beside it was a military policeman looking very alert.

There were only three lorries to stay in this area as it was a dropping-off point. Some of the men had to join another unit somewhere in Europe. This I was told later. As we joined each other inside, we were told that this was to be our billet for the night. We were to sleep, shave and get our kit sorted out, for early the next morning a train would take us to another port. Our destination was still a mystery.

To locate my room for the night, I had to climb a staircase with a dirty, old carpet on every step and on to a boarded landing. A door stood slightly ajar on my right, so I pushed it open and slowly walked inside. I know the country was still at war but the entire place was a dirty shambles. It looked like it hadn't been cleaned for weeks! I felt like going outside to dig a large hole to kip in for, believe me, I'd slept in quite a few before I had left France.

Before retiring for the night I strolled down the wide street just outside. I reckoned there was a prostitute on every corner I came to. I was still amazed at seeing no damage and still had the feeling the French did not want us here in the first place. Once in a while I could see the white helmets of the military police, walking and flicking their truncheons against the nearest object. I thought to myself, God, I wish I had joined their unit, to stay put and stop travelling from pillar to post.

We were very close to the train station, so the following morning we all congregated beside the coaches and, one by one, took a seat on the train. As the train pulled out of the station we could see a lot more of the city. To me, it seemed as if I was only riding away from the grand, old city of New York, for everything was just standing upright. Under the old bridges and through towns we went. The old train was very slow but we were getting ever closer to the port that the soldiers would soon depart from. Then the large sign appeared beside the track and the train slowly came to a halt. We had finally arrived at the port of Marseille.

We all got off the train, to stand in a group. I gazed around and was surprised that even this city had hardly suffered any damage. We had the chance to see some of the city whilst we were here, so my chum and I walked up one street and down another. Many people shouted at us in French. We were indifferent to their shouts. However, I will say that this city was far friendlier than Paris.

After a while, the two of us had to hurry back to the postal unit and head to the docks, where a large ship awaited us. It had no name on it, or at least I could not see one and I was told it used to carry rail engines during peacetime. But it did have a very prominent weapon – a .155 artillery gun on the stern – so it was always prepared for action.

The sleeping quarters for the officers were above deck and in the hold there were canvas hammocks for the soldiers. Just beside our sleeping quarters were old canvas-topped lorries with loads of other materials. On the whole, it seemed a sturdy craft.

I was not asked to volunteer, but the captain had wanted someone's help to manage the big gun and you can guess who the mug was... yours truly! The reason for my selection was because I had combat duty experience and this would keep me on my toes. I did at the time feel like putting two fingers up but then realised they were right. I did know a little about these weapons and so accepted the order. Mind you, I hadn't realised I would have no other duties to perform whilst on this journey, only to be available when required to load and fire the great gun.

We were then told to gather in a group before the officer in charge and, as we all stood at ease, he said in a loud voice: 'This is going to be a long and often unpleasant trip.' He stopped and looked in my direction, then resumed talking. 'It will at times be unbearable, as a lot of you will be seasick and wish to God you were still on dry land, but the army just cannot transport you men any other way.'

The soldier who was standing beside me leaned over to whisper in my ear, 'So it's the other part of the world?'

Then we both sat back as the officer spoke

again. 'I cannot tell you too much at this time, but the route we will travel will be through the Panama Canal and into the Pacific then, more than likely, I will be able to tell you more. Thank you.' He then walked away and as he did so we could hear the big ship's engine. We eased away from the berth and we were now on our way.

I joined the ship's gun crew and got to know all their names and became quite adept at the gun drill – I do believe we all achieved grade one on our practice runs. The ship's captain was dead right when he told the men about seasickness. I'll bet nearly everyone on this ship threw up over the ship's railings at least a dozen times!

Three days out from France, I had pains in the kidney area. It was not too bad and so I ignored it, for I believed it was just a slight strain, but the next day it seemed to get worse and I was nearly doubled up with shooting pains. I walked, with assistance, along to the sick bay and the ship's doctor told me off for not reporting to him earlier and I was ordered straight to bed.

Shortly after, land came into sight and, before long, the big ship was anchoring off Panama, to await its turn to go through the Canal. I was taken to the hospital in Panama for an examination. To my delight, they found nothing serious but I was told to report at once if the pain returned. I was quickly taken back to the ship, just in time, as it happened, for the troopship was now ready to enter the Canal.

I felt very privileged to go down this long,

winding river and to have seen the jungles on each side, with crocodiles resting on the bank, waiting for any garbage to be thrown overboard from the passing ship. Then we were in the Pacific Ocean and going over the calm, warm waters.

We were not even halfway to our destination and everyone was fed up with seeing nothing but water. Twice a day, morning and night, every soldier on-board, had to do lots of exercise, jumping up and down for twenty minutes and this sometimes went on for an hour.

I spent most of my time chatting with the gun crew and often had the odd practice run but different games would have to be thought of to keep the men from going bonkers. One of the most popular games was to blindfold two men and to put them in a ring with boxing gloves on. There were many soldiers aboard this ship who would have a gamble on which man would still be standing after half an hour, or for that matter the one who drew blood first. This game had to end, however, for it almost turned into a sad tragedy. One of the young soldiers who watched outside of the ring was smashed in the face and fell over backwards, tripping over a mooring rope. He reached for the railing but missed it and fell over the side of the ship into the Pacific. It surely must have been his lucky day, though, for as soon as he fell over the rails, shouts of 'man overboard' were heard and the ship slowly came to a halt. He only had to swim a short distance before he was hauled aboard – a very lucky soldier indeed.

Dolphins were always following behind the ship, gliding up and down off the stern and port side. We saw these creatures so often we even gave them names. Another of the spectacles was the flying fish, not actually flying but gliding just above the waves. In the morning, many of these six-inch fish were found scattered on the deck but were thrown back into the sea because they could be very dangerous if stepped on. This is why they were nicknamed 'slipper fish'. Day in and day out, there was nothing but water and more water, but at last despair turned to hope for, out of the blue, seagulls were flying above, so we all knew that land was somewhere close by and, sure enough, it was.

A short time later a voice shouted, 'Land ahoy!' and the ship slowly came to a halt. We were told that the land was part of the Solomon Islands. It was a beautiful sight but any land would have been a bonus. I had never seen an island so full of palm trees and it certainly had its share of coconuts and the odd banana tree. There were seagulls, albatrosses and I even saw a long, green lizard.

A large building was erected under the tall palms and it reminded me of an old army barrack.

This particular island was used as a supply base and many large ships were moored beside ours, awaiting fresh supplies. Two of my chums and I were the first off the ship and, as I trudged along a footpath, I sat down and removed my shoes so I could feel the earth between my toes. It had been such a long time since I'd felt the ground and I felt like a young boy again. I think everyone's morale was high. We had been nearly two weeks on the sea and this stop had been well worth the wait.

Everyone joined in with me and, barefooted, we ran like hell up the sandy beach to the wooden hut. Although none of us had any money, we were offered a cold drink, on the house. Even today I don't know what it was, but I do know it was the best damn drink I'd had in a very long time.

This was one of the memories that would stay with me for ever.

But everything was about to change, for we were soon told to report back to our vessel. All of us gathered in a big room and the major stood before a large map. He held a long cane in his left hand, which he pointed at the map.

'We are here!' The tip of his cane touched an island. 'But now look at the distance we still have to go.' He then pointed the cane at another island and a gasp was heard. 'Yes!' said the officer. 'So now you know our destination and, provided the enemy is not about, we will set up base in the vicinity of Japan, on the island of Okinawa.' He then looked around the room and said, 'If anything else does arise, you'll be informed.'

On the ship, the night was hot and humid. Then came the sound of the rusty, old anchor being raised and, at the same time, the mighty engines in the hold could be heard. I hurried up on to the deck and saw the shore lights glimmer and slowly disappear as we pulled away from the large island.

The last I saw of this quiet place was a huge ship moored beside us and it gradually vanished from view.

Day after day went by and, believe me, the life aboard this craft became extremely boring, for the same routine occurred every day. Occasionally, the soldiers were happy, but morale for the majority of the men was very low. I would make some type of excuse to go below deck to be on my own and sometimes tears would form in my eyes. Whenever this happened, I always returned to the men with a smile and put on a brave face. After all, I was supposed to be a hard, young soldier and I expect everyone believed that.

I just had to find something to do and so took what little money I could muster and played a card game called blackjack. It's not surprising that I was broke in just half an hour but I did feel a lot better, for it made me think about something else. Up until the time I was drafted into the army, I could almost always tell, when asked, what day or time it was. When in combat a soldier does not count the days, let alone what the time is, for more often than not he's fighting for his life. Time has no meaning, only daylight, then night. The soldier is always thinking, will I be alive at this time tomorrow?

This was one time when I actually felt safe during the war, for I had heard on the grapevine that the Americans had air superiority and the Japanese navy was virtually non-existent. This left only the foot soldiers of the Japanese forces to contend with. On this day, I cannot say exactly when, but it was afternoon, since the sun was just above our heads, a lot of the men were standing on the ship, looking to the northwest, suddenly had to shield their eyes from a giant flash that lit up the horizon. The soldiers then believed the flash to be a distant thunder storm, as a slight rumble was heard shortly afterwards.

We knew this was a long way off so took no more notice. An officer spoke to us the following day and we all knew it must be good news because he was smiling as he spoke.

'Today I must inform you that the Japanese forces have finally given up and have conceded defeat, so now the war is nearly over.' He started to walk away, then turned and said, 'Although I have told you this news, I would still advise extreme caution, for it will take some time before action ceases and there still may be, or will be, the odd fanatic fighting.'

The following days turned out to be nightmarish for me. I awoke from a restless sleep with pain in my kidney area. I thought I was dying. I got out of my bunk, screaming in agony. If one or two of the soldiers had not come to my aid, I'm sure I would have passed out. They asked me where the pain was and I pointed towards my back. They carefully led me to the latrines. I felt an urgent need to pass water. I urinated but only blood came out and I was being sick at the same time. In the meantime on deck, land had been sighted. At last we had arrived at a port somewhere south of Japan on the island of Okinawa.

I was taken to the base hospital, where I was carried into a large canvas-topped tent. The doctor, an officer in the medics department, stood above me with another man. 'I know the agony this pain is causing, but I'm sure you will feel better now.' He looked across at the other man and then he felt my brow saying, 'There is nothing we can do, as you have already passed the foreign matter, commonly known as gravel, through your system. This may reoccur at any time but, for now, the only way to help prevent this happening is to drink lots of water.'

The doctor was right. The pain soon disappeared but the soreness in my kidneys remained. However, this I could put up with. I was able to walk, but every so slowly, to reach my waiting transport.

We drove for about ten miles along the desolate and dusty road. The soldier driving had to pull to the side of the road, as it was getting quite dark and there were no street lights on the island. There was also still the chance of an attack. This may sound daft but there were many Japanese would sacrifice their own lives in order to kill Americans.

I can't say I had a wonderful sleep for I had to either sit up with my back against a tree or lie on my stomach and, no matter what my posture was, I still felt as sore as hell. The driver and I were well armed. He carried a pistol and my weapon was a short rifle called a carbine that was usually carried by an army officer, but neither of us expected to use them. The two of us agreed that sentries were needed, so each of us would take turns, two hours on, two hours off and he took the first shift. I was awake two hours later and got to my feet to look at the sky. It was very cloudy but a giant yellow moon every so often sent its rays between the night clouds. When this happened the earth was bathed in light and shadows, a most wonderful sight.

One hour into my shift, I noticed that two dark patches had turned into men. They seemed to be creeping towards our lorry. I very gently shook my partner's shoulder and, as he awoke, I put one of my fingers to my mouth to caution him to be quiet. The boulder that we sat beside was only a short distance from the motor. We had chosen this area because the driver thought we would be in a protected area if someone or something wanted to harm us and, as it happened, he was right.

Every time the moon went behind a cloud the men moved forward, stopping whenever it lit up the ground. Both of us knew this was happening since it was easy to see every move the two men made. Up until now we were more intent on seeing what their intentions were. Then, one of the shadows lit a match beside the lorry and both of us were ready for action.

The moon lit up the scene again and the enemy was there holding a large, burning torch. One of the men was about to throw it when we both fired our guns at the same time. The man holding the big torch dropped it, fell to the earth in a crumpled heap and lay very still. We had, however, made a small error, for we had both shot at the same man and, in doing so, saw the second man run into the shadows of the night.

Being very careful, we went and stood above the man we had shot and, sure enough, it was a man wearing a Japanese army uniform. In a way we both felt sorry for this soldier's death, though we knew that they certainly wouldn't have been sorry for ours. Thank God we had saved our transport, for if we had lost it, just look at the position we'd have been in and more than likely the dead Japanese soldier had many friends.

This encounter, though, did prove one thing to us, never to believe everything one hears. Was the war really over? Well, this, I was sure, would put us on guard until we were very certain. The huge, bright sun arose on the distant horizon and it was time to be on our way to a far away destination. I leaned back on the well-worn seat, stretched both my legs forward and closed my eyes. It felt wonderful to just rest and relax until we arrived at the postal unit.

God only knows where it was. I could not expect it to be a wonderful hotel but I could at least retire at night in safety. I am sure, though, my mate and I hoped it would be a place of security. The driver and I did not speak for a long time, for both of us felt sorry and guilty about the killing of the Japanese soldier the night before, at least the two of us had buried him and said a few words. I do believe that if I had known how cruel the Japanese had been to our men then I would not have felt so sorry.

The scenery we observed was very plain but still had an unfamiliar look to it, long glades of trees, mostly bamboo and the odd bush I had not seen before. Here and there, usually around small groups of huts and sometimes in unusual places, we saw bomb craters where artillery fire had struck.

The morning turned into late afternoon and it was then that I saw the great Pacific Ocean on my left-hand side. This depended on the route we travelled but we were always following the long coastline. Then, at long last, the jeep stopped on the top of a high hill where we had a short breather and enjoyed a C-ration for dinner and washed it down with a drink from our canteens.

Before we started on our way, the driver tapped on my arm, then pointed to something far away and, following his pointing finger, I saw in the distance, a large building. He said, 'That's our destination, it's an old seaplane hangar.' He then pointed along the coast, saying, 'The small island just beyond the hangar, is called Si Soce and the larger one next to it is Iwo Jima.' I could see how close the larger of the two islands was to where I had to work.

We were able to see the long road going down to the bottom and disappearing, before merging again some way beyond and finally could not see it any more, owing to the large hills and other obstacles. As we continued on our journey, I could not help but wonder why so few of the population were to be seen. However, at times I felt that someone was watching our every move.

Time went by and the sun was well into the sky, then just around a sharp bend was one of the prettiest buildings I'd seen in a long time, a pagoda of such beauty that it took one's breath away. The eaves of the old roof were shaped like a woman's up-turned hair and just around the square roof, it looked very old, pretty and peaceful, but very foreign. The jeep passed the pagoda and I could not resist looking back and, to my surprise, saw at least seven or eight Japanese peasants hiding behind obstacles and shaking their fists at us.

As we approached a bend in the road, a stout man dressed in a black robe and brandishing a large, pointed stick appeared. I saw him raise his arms forming a 'V' shape and more hidden men came out to stand just beside him. He then raised his arms to shout but we had not waited around long enough to hear him, for we had turned the corner of the road. There may have been lots of trouble if we had stopped to admire this old pagoda and, who knows, our chance of reaching our destination could have been nil.

The sun was near the horizon but would not set for at least a couple of hours and so the young man driving the jeep said, 'Why not close your eyes for a while, as we still have quite a distance to go.'

I closed my eyes and then I was dreaming. I'd had nightmares before but I'll always remember this dream because it felt so real. A large bird came from overhead, swooped down and wrapped its talons around me, but as I looked up it wasn't a bird at all, it was a human being, but covered in feathers. It carried me over a giant stretch of water. I was trying to get away from this creature but all at once it opened its talons. I plummeted down and down and all the time I was screaming.

Then, as I was just about to hit the earth, I awoke with someone shaking me. There was a soldier looking at me in utter amazement. Thank God, I was with the living again. Most of my dreams have had some type of meaning to them but this one I could not explain.

Our vehicle stopped just opposite Si Soce and thus I knew we had but a few more miles to travel. Then over a small hill and on to a straight road, the lorry pulled up beside the large hangar and stopped. I was with my postal unit again. Not long after we arrived, a group of my friends led me to a house beside the hangar and told me to choose a bunk. They would give me more information in the morning after I had reported to the officer in charge.

I knew the moment I lay on my bunk that I was amongst friends and would have a peaceful sleep. I closed my eyes and within seconds was in a deep sleep. I believe this was to be one of the best I'd had in a long time. I awoke the following morning a little late, hastily got dressed and was just about to go when I noticed three green-coloured lizards crawling on the old rafters just above the door. I had heard about these creatures before and was told that they changed colours to blend in with the surrounding scenery.

This was exactly what they did, for as I opened the door to go out they had disappeared from view.

I found a soldier in the next room, who told me where I was to find the officer in charge. I was to go through the door of our sleeping quarters, then around it and in front of me would be the postal hangar, then go forward, turn right and enter the first door. I followed these instructions and left the sleeping quarters.

It was not the postal unit that made me stop, it was the beautiful Pacific Ocean spread out before my eyes. Being such a sunny morning, I also saw the long, brown road disappearing into the far distance. It looked like a huge snake. I raised my eyes from the sea to see the two islands appear – these were the two we had seen the previous night. These two pieces of land, nestling in the calm ocean, looked exactly like a vision of paradise but I was to learn later it was more a part of hell. The room the officer was sitting in was quite small. I could see him looking at a handful of papers. The door to his room was half open and, just before I knocked, he beckoned me in.

I hastily walked in and stood to attention, saluting as I did so. The captain returned my salute and said, 'At ease, Corporal. I told the men to let you have a lie in as I thought you might need it.' He looked down at some paper on his desk and spoke again. 'Be at ease, soldier and take heed of what I say. I have your army records here and have noted some of the deeds you have performed or achieved in Europe, which is why you were picked for this unit.' Pausing for breath, he continued.

'The postal unit site had been set up during your sickness and is now ready to collect and deliver, for the war is officially over with Japan but we still must be on the alert. Therefore, I have just asked the sergeant to work collectively with you for I still believe we should have a security system at all times. Now, will you accept this post, Corporal?'

'Yes, sir,' I said, saluting as I left.

We set up a rota for sentry duty to guard twenty-four hours a day. After a few days the security had been sorted out and everyone in the camp had certain orders to follow. Every so often my past would return to haunt me and sometimes I had my usual nightmares, but I would try to keep myself busy by doing a bit of mail sorting.

During one of my quieter moments in the postal hangar, I picked up a letter and, by chance, read the address. To my amazement, it was addressed to my home town in the USA. I then looked at the return address and it was from a regiment not too many miles away from this postal unit. The soldier fighting there was a close friend of mine, someone I had gone to school with and grown up with. Twice this had happened in my travels in the army, once in Europe after I was wounded and now in Okinawa.

I located the sergeant, told him what I had found and asked him to cover for me. Without any hesitation he told me, 'Take all the time you need, my friend.' I was not sure about the exact location of the place but had a rough idea of where it was. There was such a regiment located just a few miles inland, almost opposite Iwo Jima. We had received a few letters from the area and so this was the location I had to get to. The problem was I had no transport. There was no way I would be able to walk that far, so I would have to find something with four wheels on it. I did not have a jeep at my disposal and so would have to pinch or borrow one. There were many of these army jeeps about and so finding one was quite easy. There was one just across the road and it even had a key in the ignition.

It was like taking candy from a baby, for I got in and drove it off. I drove through many small villages, occasionally without seeing anyone but with the feeling that there were eyes watching me. The early morning passed quickly into noon. To my left, I saw a group of soldiers all sitting down and looking damn tired, in fact they all looked as if they had just been in a fight. I asked one of the soldiers if he would direct me to a certain platoon in a regiment and to my utter surprise he informed me it was the one I had entered. Then I asked if he knew a soldier in the platoon called Albert Richards and without hesitation, he pointed to a man sitting with his back to a tree.

I walked over to stand in front of the tree the soldier had pointed to. The man who I looked at certainly was my friend of old and he appeared to be asleep, for the helmet he wore lay tilted against the tree and his eyes were closed. As I looked down at Albert, I understood the tiredness and stress he had been going through for I also had been walking in hell and knew only too well how he was feeling. Albert had not shaved for God knows how long and looked to me as if he had just fallen out of a large garbage bin. As I lay my hand on his shoulder, he opened his eyes and I saw the fear and stress as he looked at me.

'God, Buddy, is that you?' he spoke in a whisper. 'Or am I dreaming again?'

My chum pushed his helmet aside, sat upright and beckoned me to sit just beside him. This I did and he grasped my hand ever so forcefully. 'How did you find me and what the hell are you doing in this godforsaken place?'

'It's a long story, my friend. To start with, I found the return address on an envelope addressed to your own family in Camden and had to look you up.' Private Richards closed his eyes.

'Buddy, we parted long ago and went our separate ways, so I never thought I would see your face again.' He opened his eyes to continue. 'I dare say we have both been to hell, only yours was in another part of the world, but at least we were able to walk out again with God's help.'

I stayed with my friend for the best part of the day and learned many things about the Japanese and that they were known as 'gooks' – a nickname given to these islanders, who were seen as wicked, cruel people and regarded as barely human. He also told me how the Japanese treated prisoners of war and described to me the battles he had taken part in.

I felt extremely grateful I had ended up in

Europe fighting the Germans, instead of in Japan fighting the Japanese. The bright sun had begun to get near the horizon and so it was time for me to go. Before doing so, Albert told me that all of his regiment had occupied Iwo Jima and talked me through many battles. 'I would say to you, my dear friend, if you ever have the chance, get some transport and visit those two islands and imagine what took place there.'

We both shook hands, had a hug and parted company. Waving to him I got back in the jeep and drove off, thinking to myself, at least I've met two of my old school chums and with any luck we shall meet again.

The bright sun gradually went over the horizon and twilight bathed the old earth. I made it back to my unit just before the moon's yellow rays sent shadows here and there. Parking the borrowed jeep exactly where I had found it, I felt I had achieved something extra special on this day. My next visit would be to the sergeant and so hastily I knocked on his door. We talked for a long time and I was able to tell him about parts of the island he had not seen and the finding of my close friend. He got to his feet and, opening the door, said, 'Goodnight, Corporal, see you in the morning.'

Resting in my bunk that night, I thought of all the day's events and, long before I got half way through them, I'd fallen into a sound, dreamless sleep.

The Eye of the Storm

Early next morning, I awoke very early, for I had to check that everything had gone according to plan whilst I was absent, but no complaints were made. Having been told that everything was in order, I wandered down to the beach and was soon joined by another PFC John. It was such a wonderful day and the Pacific Ocean was as calm as a millpond.

There was white, foamy surf as it reached the sandy shoreline. Looking out to sea, I was able to see the two big islands. They looked so close, one felt as though one could reach out and touch them. This was because of the heat of the day. In fact, two of them were quite a distance from us, at least a mile. It was then I remembered what Albert had told me: 'If possible, you must see the two islands, to see what has happened there.'

As this was to be a day of rest, being a Sunday, John and I sat down to figure out what we would do to pass the time, maybe going to the two islands if it could be accomplished. There were just two options... by boat or raft. But where the dickens would we find a craft suitable for this silly mission? We watched a seagull settle on the sea and I think we had the same idea, so we both started to search for wood.

We searched all along the clean, white beach, finding only a small collection of wood, nowhere near the amount needed to make a raft but we did find two long bits that would be good for paddles. The two of us were almost ready to give up when I spotted something out of the ordinary and then our prayers were answered. It was lying just above the sands. The hangar had been used as a seaplane building and what we had found was a pontoon, shaped like a small canoe that was used for landing on water. This was just the ticket for our journey to the islands.

Looking back on this crackpot idea, I would say we were both mad but the younger a man is the more likely he will go where angels fear to tread. Without further ado, we took the two long paddles, dragged the pontoon down near the water and began searching for two seats. These were soon found, as well as two old pails in case we had to bail out any water. The pontoon was then gently pushed into the sea and we got into it. We were both so pleased at the way it gracefully moved through the low swells of the ocean. Eyeing the water I said, 'OK, skipper!' and without knowing what lay ahead, we paddled the pontoon towards the distant island.

The island of Si Soce looked like paradise. The nearer we got the more beautiful it became, for the white sands of the huge beach blended with the green of the trees. Just before we reached the beach, John and I saw movement in the trees and then, upon looking closer, saw people were looking at us.

The tide and a breeze swept us slightly sideways as we reached the water's edge. We again looked for the faces but they had disappeared and there seemed to be nothing but greenery. Having seen these people, it made us hesitate and to wonder if it was worth the risk to explore this big island as well as Iwo Jima. The latter could be seen in the distance, should we take another chance and explore Si Soce or just go to Iwo Jima, our intended destination?

Many a mistake is made in one's life and we were about to make another but this one I must admit was because we wanted a break from paddling and my bum sure was aching. We beached the pontoon and carried it to just above the waterline, where the trees were spread along the top of the beach. At long last, we reached the edge of the trees and sat down beside a tree trunk. We noticed quite a few of the trees were bent inland, probably because of the mighty winds coming from the sea.

We found a path leading into the trees. Looking left and right I was amazed at the different types of plants and greenery – just the place for an ambush! I looked at John, who carried no weapon – not even a rubber slingshot – but I was carrying a light carbine rifle. As we walked along, we felt danger was close by.

John and I tried to shake this dread off and at long last we entered a small, open field. I imagine we were approaching the middle of the island, for the centre of this wide opening was quite large. We saw quite a few thatched houses. All looked very much alike and each roof had grey straw on top. Coming out of the door of each house, Japanese villagers appeared, some with long sticks in their hands and certainly none were smiling as they came towards us.

The group was about three hundred yards before us when we heard loud noises at the rear and turning we saw more men coming out of the trees. We did at least make it to the woods but John was flung to the ground and a dirty, bearded old man came at him with a knife. Without thinking or hesitating, I shot him, leaving John free to jump up. I fired my carbine at anything that moved, even at those coming towards us from the houses.

I believe they never realised we had a weapon, so this certainly gave us a slight advantage. We were able to reach the trees but from behind us came the loud noises of pursuit. Following the pathway until it ended, we rushed out of the leafy woods and were lucky on two counts. The tide had come in and the pontoon was resting on the waterline – so if we had turned up a few minutes later, it could have floated away and without it we would have perished at the hands of the angry villagers.

We had the pontoon afloat and were sitting in it just as the locals broke out of the undergrowth, shaking their fists and shouting blue murder. Every one I saw had either a big club or a thin, long-bladed knife. After this close shave, it was decided that our next port of call would be Iwo Jima. We both realised how lucky we were to have got off this island alive but, as we drew away from Si Soce, we put the past behind us and paddled on.

The sun was blazing down upon us and I could not help but think of childhood memories, of the day I used the top of a trunk for a boat and the times my mum smacked my bum for falling into the dirty, stinking frog pond. Then I heard John shouting, and then gesticulating with one hand, and this brought me back to reality for, as I followed his finger, I saw the black fins just above the water. If I had not been daydreaming, I would have spotted them sooner but from the calm ocean came a school of tiger sharks and they were swimming all around our pontoon.

God, now another problem was with us. This species of shark was known to attack anything that moved above water and would be even more dangerous than the mighty whites. We both put down our paddles and sat very still, hoping and praying that our silence and stillness would make them search for other prey. Over an hour passed (it seemed like years) but the tiger sharks still circled the pontoon, always getting nearer and nearer.

We realised that, if one of these sharks nudged or surfaced from beneath the craft, we would have been certain goners. The boat was drifting with the currents, bobbing up and down because the tides were always changing, but all the time we were drifting towards Iwo Jima island. Then the situation became critical, for the sharks came even closer. I leaned a little to the side and actually touched the black fin, which felt like leather and looked at John as he pointed to the gun, he had fear in his eyes. I knew that without some type of action from us, we would end up as shark food.

Gently reaching down, I lifted the carbine and raised it from the bottom of the boat but found to my dismay that it was quite wet. I opened my legs and found that my carbine had been sitting in water. The pontoon had begun to leak. It was now imperative that we reach land as soon as possible. I held the rifle in my lap and dried it with my shirtsleeve, then I took a clip of ammunition, blew down the barrel and loaded the carbine. There were not many clips left because we had used quite a few on Si Soce. The black dorsal fin broke the surface three yards away and, in one motion, I aimed and fired and saw the slight ripple of water as the bullet hit it just below the fin. Nothing happened and so I fired a second round at another fin.

Then John yelled, 'You've hit the bastard!' and I could see in one spot of the ocean the water had turned red and before our eyes the sharks seemed to disappear. My strategy seemed to have worked for I'm sure the tiger sharks had followed their wounded friend and were now busy having a feast.

We started to paddle away from this hell hole as fast as we could.

John and I reached Iwo Jima shortly afterwards and carried the pontoon from the sea on to the sand, but before we explored the island some repairs had to be made to stop the leak. The small hole in the pontoon was quickly mended. It had a slight crack and the welding had opened a little, so we pushed a piece of my shirt into the opening. The two of us had been so damn eager to get our feet on to solid ground, that neither of us had given a lot of thought to what we would find inland. The small cove was sandy and situated well below the huge boulders with spaces between them and all types of seaweed and wood were strewn upon the white sands.

We left the boat and slowly made our way up amongst the huge rocks and then came to an abrupt stop, for all around us there lay American army gear. I counted twelve M1 rifles and a helmet that lay under an overhanging rock. Then I noticed a glimmer of light coming from an object on the white sands and bent down to pick it up. In the palm of my hands was a pair of dog tags (metallic disks worn around a soldier's neck for identity purposes). I put these in my pocket to hand in when we returned to our unit. In total, we found fifteen M1 rifles, nine helmets and lots of clothing, some of it ripped into shreds but there were no bodies. God knows there must have been quite a few casualties, for even the grey-black rocks had dried blood on them.

We still had to make our way through the rocky boulders to reach the faraway headland. So carrying a load of army weapons with us was out of the question but we didn't want to just leave them, so when we reached the high, rock-strewn ground, the rifles were thrown into the Pacific Ocean. This was an extremely barren island.

It could never be compared to its sister, Si Soce, for whereas the island we had just left had trees and lots of green and fauna, this island had none. It would have been nice to have seen what this piece of land had looked like before the war but now literally everything had been destroyed. The bombing and artillery shells from the great armada of ships had cleared Iwo Jima of all its vegetation and to make sure of victory, the army of soldiers had gone ashore and finished the job.

Everywhere John and I went, there were many signs of human suffering and many a savage scar had been left upon mother earth. Where the islanders had lived, now there were deep craters. All around were human remains. The smell of death still floated on the air. The sun rose high into the blue of the cloudless sky and Okinawa could be seen shimmering in the distance.

The two of us were following the long coastline and looking over the hills. Earth was jutting out from the land to form a large, U-shaped pattern and it was on this piece of land where we decided to rest. The huge, black boulder we sat on was high above and overlooking the mighty Pacific Ocean and if either of us had taken a step forward he would have fallen into the water below.

'What do you make of that, John?' I pointed to the bottom of the rock we sat on. 'Surely this can't be what it looks like? If I was to guess, I would say it was a partially submerged jeep.' But to make doubly sure, we moved to a spot nearer the object. It was a large disposal dump and it certainly was a jeep, with many other items, including seven or eight torpedo boats dumped in a pile beneath the water. We presumed it was just cheaper to get rid of gear this way than to have it transported back to North America.

Time was flying by, so we hurried to make up the time we had lost earlier, for we wanted to see and explore as much of this island as possible. Every twist and turn on the walks around this piece of land produced what we had expected to see but here and there was evidence of fierce battles. We had searched only half of this large island and then a discovery was made. Large holes could be seen in the sandy earth, but to our surprise tunnels had been dug to connect one cave to another.

The first and only hole I climbed into was a place of horror. The earth outside was black and on the inside I found three bodies, as black as the dirt outside. I then realised how all these people had died, for in basic training we had used one of these very deadly weapons and knew the destruction it could cause. It was a liquid gas flamethrower. To be killed by a rifle bullet was very quick but to be burned alive like this was deplorable.

I then realised, of course, that this was wartime and the only way to remove somebody from inside the earth was to use the flamethrower. As we went from one area to another, the large caverns had black corpses lying both in and outside and the stench of death was everywhere. I felt sick of all this slaughter and I also felt pity, but I knew that when fighting the enemy, no quarter could be given.

Many a mother and child were doomed to die on this damn island because no one knew if there were soldiers hiding below the earth and no chances could be taken. We left this area of holes and passing by the last one, sat down on a small hill. As I gazed back at the bodies outside the blackened holes, I thought to myself, I'm glad I was not given a flamethrower. If I had used one, thoughts of doing so would have stayed with me my whole life. Of course, I have my own cross to carry, so I had a feeling I knew what any soldier felt for carrying and using it, though he too would find life goes on. The nightmares become less frequent but a soldier never forgets. Whilst I was meditating, my eyes focused on the hazy land in the distance and I realised that we had to make our way back to the pontoon. The sun was riding very close to the horizon and before long it would be twilight. In my reckoning, we had about three hours to get back.

Without looking back, John and I walked slowly along the way we had come and I believe neither of us wanted to spend the night on this godforsaken piece of land. There was a slight mishap on the return trip for I fell into one of the numerous holes, falling head over heels and landing on top of a putrefied body. But John helped me out and, although I had a slight sprain, I was able to limp back to our craft and boy were we glad to see it. The tide was well in and so we had no need to carry the pontoon out to the water.

We floated the boat and had a difficult time getting into it but, once settled, started to paddle towards Okinawa. It had been a wonderful adventure to explore the two islands. Even if it had been a stupid thing to do, I would have done it all over again for it was something we would always remember. Without mishap, we landed on the home island and turned to make our way back to the postal hangar.

Later, as I lay on my bunk and stared at the wooden rafters, I could see a large spider spinning his silken web and, as I watched, a fly flew into the silken trap and, just as the long, black spider grabbed it, I fell into a deep sleep but instead of sleeping like a log the same old nightmare returned, only this time it was worse. All I saw were dead bodies walking towards me. As I turned to run away, I found myself being shaken by something, then awoke, seeing the sentry staring at me.

'Where the hell do you think you're going and who are you?' he said, brandishing his M1 rifle. He poked me again and I looked around me. God, I was sleepwalking. I was indeed lucky, for I could easily have been shot by the sentry. Once he knew who I was, he sent me on my way.

The sun was just coming over the horizon and a private stood above me with a written message to report to the sergeant's quarters as soon as possible. He was waiting just inside the door and, as I entered, he took me by the arm and led me to a chair. 'I've had a report from one of the sentries about the affair last night. I do believe, corporal, that a check-up from a doctor would be advisable, do you not agree?' I thanked him for his concern and, without delay, a jeep was sent and I was taken to see a medic.

The army doctor gave me all types of tests and when he was satisfied a verdict was given. I was taken into a room and the medic said, 'Corporal, I have come to the conclusion that you are quite fit in body but your mind is still unsettled and you still have a stress problem. I'll send my report off to the officer in charge and recommend a few days leave.' Saluting him, I turned and left the room.

The following days passed slowly and this gave me the opportunity to further explore the island and take as much time as I needed, but it was the long, dark nights that I dreaded. The trip to the army doctor had not helped, nearly every night I closed my eyes the visions seemed to return and the sleepwalking became more regular. Believe me, at times I felt like ending it all. It was after one of those nights that I got out of bed in the morning and decided I would go for a long drive to pass the time and do something different.

Over one hill and down the other I went and the longer I drove the better I felt. The migraine I'd had the night before disappeared and at long last I felt my old self again. A few miles on, I parked the jeep and strolled along the road to stretch my legs. Before long it became twilight and then darkness.

The large, pale moon rose above the earth and looked so close that I felt I could touch it. The light from above bathed the earth and showed a huge battle had taken place here, leaving pieces of clothing and lots of other objects behind. Then I noticed something glinting, so I bent over and picked it up. To my surprise, it was two dog tags. Once before this incident had occurred, on the two islands we had explored, and now here on Okinawa. The chain on the tags was slightly tarnished but the embossed words read 'PFC E Carter'.

Again, I searched the area where I had found the pair of tags and, just beyond my feet, was a small, brown book. I held it in my left hand. It read… 'Given to Ernie Carter'. The book was The Bible.

The time was getting on so I returned to the jeep and drove away. Arriving late at night, I went straight to bed.

I will now describe what our army living quarters looked like and what the surrounding area was composed of. Taking into account that peace had only just been declared, there were really only the bare essentials.

Outside our quarters and in a small pagoda-like shed, a generator was situated. This was where our supply of electricity came from and this damn machine was on the go for twenty-four hours a day. There was no running water, which meant no flushing toilets and this reminded me of my childhood days, when we had an outside toilet.

When I was a boy, my dad dug a hole six feet long, three feet wide and about four feet deep. He put a long, wide piece of flat wood, with a round hole cut in the middle, to sit on but, of course, it was erected like a bench inside a shack with a door. So, you see, the toilet on Iwo Jima was based on the same principle.

A tree stem with a 'Y' in it was pounded into the ground on both sides of the deep trench and a nine-foot pole was laid across the ditch to rest in the 'Y'. It was a testing time for a soldier as he sat over the pole, if he slipped it would have been his downfall. The other hazards he faced were the enormous bluebottle flies, I swear they were as large as birds. A soldier would sit with a branch off a Di bush (a short round, leafy shrub), to hit the bluebottle flies but it never seemed to work.

Beside the toilet, there lay a large, brownish mound of earth, almost as tall as a house and to the left of it was a cluster of brick-shaped rocks, forming a door. About fifteen or twenty bricks had been disturbed and lay in a heap on the ground.

Above the door could be seen words of a sort,

but I was not able to read them since they were in Japanese but later on I was told that the islanders had put a curse on anyone who disturbed the dead by entering the crypt. I did not feel frightened by this. I had a curse put on me when I was drafted into the army and if it had not been for my guardian angel, I would have been amongst the dead a long time ago. However, I did not have any intention of crawling between bricks and entering it, for God only knew what would be found on the inside.

A full week later, the army doctor advised me to take things easy but I would be able to do small chores, providing there was no stress involved. The days and weeks seemed to fly by and, as each week came to an end, I made sure I wrote to my lovely wife in England. As time went by, I began to feel like my old self again, so much so that I was able to help the sergeant with sentry duty and in my spare time do odd jobs around the unit. Many days later, after a well-deserved sleep, I awoke, washed, had my breakfast and strolled down to the beach. I had plenty of time as work did not start for another hour, so being in no hurry, I sat down on the sands.

Over the placid sea, I saw Iwo Jima and there seemed to be a hazy mist so dense it covered the highest part of the island and, as I observed, it sparkled here and there like a diamond. The quiet was incredible – not a sound could be heard and the few seagulls seen earlier had all disappeared, leaving the shoreline void and empty. I arose to walk towards the hangar, meeting all the day staff as they were entering the postal unit.

Rejoining my friends, I hesitated briefly, to look back at the ocean. I noticed that the sky looked very black.

Halfway through the morning shift, the officer dismissed at least three quarters of the postal staff, as the weather had deteriorated, leaving four of us to clear up. A short time later the officer came back and quietly spoke to me.

'I do not want to alarm anyone, Corporal, but if this damn wind becomes any stronger, you have my permission to clear out.' He waved to the others and walked out the door. It was about an hour later when we began to hear funny creaking noises coming from the upright structures and vibrations of metal rubbing together. It did not take long to realise that something bad was about to happen.

The four of us stood one behind the other and slowly opened the door. It came off its hinges, almost taking me with it and flew down the road. We had all fallen to the dirt floor and there was deathly fear etched onto every face, for we all knew that something had to be done quickly or we would perish. The long, wide building shook, and shuddered in the wind, rising two inches off its solid foundation. We pulled a long pole that the mail bags hung from and threw it like a lance towards the porch on the old house opposite our open door. God was with us that day, for the end rested on the bottom of the upright wooden beam, allowing us the chance to get from the fragile hangar to the solid house opposite, a chance we had to take.

Each man clutched the thin, wooden lance and began crawling hand over hand, to finally disappear into the house opposite us. I remember yelling, 'For Christ's sake, get a move on!' All the soldiers got safely into the house and so now it was my turn. I got about three quarters of the way across when the damn hangar I had just left jumped from its foundation and flew like a bird into the air.

Still clinging to the pole, I was flung like a long, wriggling snake along the ground and, luckily for me, I hit the side of the crypt and ended up inside. It took me quite a long time to realise where I was. I was finally able to pull myself together, despite all my aches and pains. I could hardly see anything, for it was as dark as night in there. I was not interested in where I was, only in thanking God that I was in one piece and still breathing, even though the air was not exactly fresh!

It was a long time before I was able to look outside. I felt as if a bus had run over me and was in great pain. I wanted to know what had happened. Very slowly, I crawled to the side of the open bricks and what came into my view were the two islands in the Pacific. I then looked for the hangar and, to my astonishment, it was not to be seen anywhere, it had literally disappeared and only part of the foundations remained.

My vision was limited but I also saw a large ocean-going ship grounded well above the waterline and some of its crew were trying to escape the winds but to no avail and a few were swept out to sea. The strong scent of death was everywhere in the crypt but I knew some of it was coming from outside, even though there were gale-force winds. I felt safe and would have to put up with the putrid smell coming from the stack of bones neatly piled on a shelf in the corner of the tomb. I saw letters painted on the dark wall but was not interested, for I had seen them before, but presumed they told of the burial chamber and named the dead Japanese.

The wind made funny noises as it hissed past the opening in the bricks and I found myself uttering the Lord's Prayer and wishing I had found refuge somewhere else. I told myself to remain calm, because nothing lasts for ever. Nearly all day I lay against the damp, slimy wall of the crypt, only to move occasionally because of cramp and to wonder how long this ordeal would last. Just like the flick of a switch, all noise from outside suddenly stopped and I thought to myself, thank God for that, but just as I thought this the winds started to blow again, only much stronger than before. Then, I realised I must have been in the eye of the hurricane.

The winds howled and the smell inside this cold, black crypt seemed to get stronger and, with the blackness and the sickly odour, I must have passed out. When I finally awoke I found myself lying at the bottom of the pile of bones. Rising to my feet, very unsteadily, I limped over to the holes in the bricks to look outside. Several of my soldier friends stood gazing at the debris that laid everywhere. They all shouted as they saw me crawl out of the side of the crypt, for they already had me down as being one of the missing, so when they saw me emerge it was like seeing a ghost. I certainly had been as close to a spirit as any soldier could be but I really howled in agony as the men touched me, proving to them I was still alive and kicking.

This hurricane was reported to have had winds of over 120 miles per hour and countless lives were lost, including those of two of my best friends. The postal unit lost everything, the mail sorted the day before must have flown halfway across the Pacific. This certainly would be classed as air mail! Literally everything not tied down just blew away. A few days after the storm we were nearly back to normal. The army engineers were called in to try to erect some type of building for the letters to be sent and collected from and, as this took quite a while to do, the officer in charge gave the men three days of leave.

Most of the men chose to rest, swim or lie on the beach every day. John and I equipped ourselves to go for a long walk, to see more parts of the island of Okinawa. We had heard through the grapevine that, as the war had ended, many soldiers would now be sent home for discharge, according to the number of points he had earned. Both of us knew this might be the only chance we had of seeing a bit more of the island.

Walking, and resting when tired, late afternoon soon arrived. During all this time, we saw no one, not even an animal. Surely there must be someone around? Then we had an uncanny feeling that someone was watching our every move, but where the hell were they? This made us nervous, for we knew that the Japanese were very good at camouflage.

As the war was declared over, after the two atomic bombs were dropped, everyone had hopes that no more killing would take place. We had been told this many times but taken nothing for granted. We also knew, beyond a shadow of a doubt, that a number of Japanese ex-servicemen would reunite and fight to the death. Sitting beside a large, moss-covered boulder and resting our backs against another rock we heard sounds of someone talking in Japanese just beyond where we sat. John looked at me and pointed as two children emerged holding hands.

The children confronted us, as children do and they got bolder, their talk louder. I lay my carbine on the ground, just in front of my boots. Their talking ceased as I reached into my pocket. The youngsters' faces showed fear and they turned to run away. I produced two bars of hard chocolate and offered it to them. They still looked uneasy, so I pointed at the object and then pointed at my mouth as if I were about to eat it. The two of them started to giggle, bowed to me and then accepted the two bars. John and I did not expect to get any information from these two and so we walked away.

The sun was just about to dip out of sight and so we stopped for the night. The place we selected had one good advantage, there was only one way in. We slept safely.

The tossing of a coin decided who would stand guard on the first shift. John lost the toss and so, armed with my carbine, he took the first watch. I lay back with my head against a tree and before anyone could say 'Jack Robinson' I was in a deep sleep.

When I awoke, I saw my chum bending over me. Getting to my feet and taking the rifle, I then took my turn. Whilst walking and looking here and there, I thought of the Japanese children and the way they had gobbled up those candy bars. It must have been the first candy they had tasted in a long time and they really seemed to enjoy eating it, for they sucked their fingers with gusto.

An old tree with a large trunk was close to where we stood, so I went to sit beneath it, leaving John lying just below me and I watched him as he snored softly. I closed my eyes and in a flash my mind was on my shy, young bride and our unborn child. I had written many letters to Joyce and had enjoyed many in return. I started to count the days and weeks that had gone by since I had last seen her lovely face and realised it must have been at least eight months.

Soon I would be a proud dad and wasn't that something to hoot about, being a father at the ripe, old age of twenty-one!

I don't know what it was but something I heard

snapped me back to reality. As I opened my eyes, I saw two figures and then two more. As the cloud passed away from the moon, it revealed four men. It didn't take me long to realise that these men were not my friends for the way they moved was sinister, spelling trouble we could ill afford. Whilst thinking of what to do next, John awoke, flung his arms into the air and shouted.

The moon came from behind a cloud, bathing the scenery in pale light, before John could yell again I shouted, 'Get down, you fool!' as gunshots could be heard in the fresh morning air. Bedlam raged on the path below me and John fell out of sight as the three Japanese soldiers threw themselves off the pathway into some bushes. One Japanese soldier was left lying face down on the ground with his weapon just beside him.

I sighed with relief as I saw John appear. Raising an arm to wave, I saw a smile on his face. My friend saw me put one finger to my mouth and then wave him to the ground. On the horizon, above the trees, the sun rose and still I waited. A short time later, what I had hoped for happened. Just opposite from where the dead Japanese soldier was located, a uniformed soldier cautiously crawled from beneath a huge bush. Lying on his stomach, he looked left, then right and, a few moments later, motioned his friends to join him.

At long last, the three Japanese soldiers were standing over their dead comrade. One of them picked up the rifle and all three of them started to chatter to each other – all this time they must have thought that the enemy had left the scene. Now was the time for John and I to fight and they were certainly taken by surprise. I had no intention of killing them, for I had enough killing on my conscience and could not stand the heartache any more.

I'm not bragging when I say I was able to hit anything I aimed at up to 300 yards. I was given an award for rifle marksmanship called the Expert Infantry Combat Badge. Motioning John to stand, I fired my first shot at the soldier holding the rifle who fell over backwards, clutching his foot. Before he hit the ground, the second soldier had thrown his gun down. As it landed, a white flag fluttered from the third man's arm and all of them were shouting and waving their arms in the air.

When we came out of hiding, we approached the three men. Somehow this capture did not seem right, for I had been told it was a blessing for a Japanese soldier to die in battle and a disgrace if he gave himself up. John held my carbine and I inspected the wounded man. He was not badly hurt, for anyone can live with a big toe missing. We put a bandage on the gash and he stood up. The other two were bowing to us and kept on whispering to each other in Japanese. As I walked up to them, they put their arms above their heads, ready to be searched. The last Japanese soldier refused to have a body search. At the time I didn't know why but I pushed him to the ground and pulled a photograph from his tightly buttoned pocket.

What could any Japanese prisoner hide that was so important? As I looked at the photograph, the man's eyes had a misty look about them, a tear formed and dropped to the ground. The photograph showed a family of four, two young children and two smiling adults. The man who was lying in front of me was the woman's husband. He very slowly put a dirty hand forward to gently take it back from my hand, stepping back as he did so.

Three courses of action could be taken. One, we could shoot them, but that would have been murder, so it was ruled out. Two, we could take them back to be tried by the military police but God knows what kind of punishment they would have received. So John and I chose the third option and set them free.

We made the Japanese sit on the ground before us. Three of their rifles with bayonets were broken in two by hitting them with a large rock and the last was taken by John as a keepsake. One hour later we were on our way back to the camp, stopping to rest and eat what little food we had left, washing it down with what remained of the water in our canteens.

I had been following the coastline of the Pacific Ocean, quite a distance from the water. We knew that sooner or later we would arrive back at the postal unit, providing, of course, it had been suitably rebuilt! After a while, we stopped and sat under an overhanging cliff that blocked out the sun's rays. It created a massive shaded area. We looked at the calmness of the waves and saw the fins of tiger sharks break the surface here and there. Soon, a rumbling sound could be heard coming from above us.

Looking up above the overhanging rock, it seemed as if the whole damn cliff was going to fall on us. Again my guardian angel was with us, for a cave was situated just behind where we were sitting and this was to be our salvation. We dived into the cave, just making it inside before the rocks hit us. The noise of the rockslide was deafening. When the dust settled, we dug our way out and at long last emerged safe and sound.

We heard laughter echoing down from above us. Then both of us looked above the rockslide. We had every reason to believe this had been planned and was no accident. Had this been our fault for letting the Japanese go free? Well, John and I will never know, but at least we were unharmed. The two of us waded into the ocean until the warm water reached our necks. Splashing and leaping up and down, we soon made all the dirt disappear and felt clean again. The most enjoyable thing was sitting on the pale sands and being dried by the pleasant warm breeze.

One hour later, the road we had left came into view and I believe the both of us yelled, 'Hip hip hurray!' Our camp was just beyond the next hill. Twilight came as we strolled into the perimeters of the postal unit and approaching us was the sergeant, whose first words were, 'Where the hell have the two of you been?' but he didn't utter those words in anger. He just put a hand on my shoulder and led me a few yards away from John.

'Now put me in the picture,' he said 'for we were beginning to think that the two of you were dead.'

I described what had occurred and about the capture of the Japanese. Suddenly, the sergeant interrupted me and said, 'By the book, those Japanese soldiers should have been brought back to camp but I suppose they would have been a liability and so what you two did was probably right.' He then turned to walk away, hesitated and then looked back, saying, 'Oh and by the way, there is a letter for you and the officer asked to see you at eight o'clock tomorrow morning. I have also been asked to tell you not to be late.'

Without delay, I saw one of the duty soldiers and he gave me the letter, and walking to my quarters, I quickly opened it. Many a letter I'd received had been from my wife and this one was urgent for she would shortly be a mother and may already have been one.

Whilst I was reading I just could not believe how fast time had flown by. I had arrived on the soils of Okinawa in September of 1945 and it was hard to believe that I hadn't seen my wife for almost nine months, as this baby was conceived on our honeymoon. Therefore I could have been a father already! That night, lying on my bunk, I just couldn't get to sleep. I kept asking myself 'Why the hell did the US government send me to Okinawa from England?' After putting my life on the line making the D-Day landing on Omaha Beach, I felt as if I had been let down by the army but then realised they knew nothing about my wife being pregnant and I often wondered if they would have taken any notice.

Eventually, I fell into slumberland and once again had one of my ugly dreams. I had the feeling of being dragged to the ground and being held there, lashing out and opening my eyes as I did so. Then I saw one of my chums appear, holding his nose which looked broken. He lisped as he spoke and held his long, pointed nose.

'By God, Buddy, you've been having a real nasty nightmare,' said one of the other soldiers, pulling me to my feet and then helping me back on my bunk. I tossed about in bed for a long time but eventually fell into a deep sleep, much to the relief of the rest of the other soldiers. The dark hours soon passed.

Upon my awakening, I washed and got dressed early since the captain had told me not to be late. I walked to headquarters and knocked. As the door opened I heard, 'Please enter,' and when I walked forward I heard the wall clock chime several times.

The officer sitting behind the desk smiled at me as I saluted. 'I believe you wanted to see me, sir,' I said and then stood to attention. He motioned me to be at ease.

'Take a seat, Corporal Nelson,' he said. 'It's not often I get the chance to have a man-to-man talk with my staff but have been told many stories about the battles you've taken part in and the blood that was shed on the Omaha Beach landing.' He looked down at some papers on his desk and continued.

'After learning all of this from your sergeant, I felt it was my duty to meet you personally.' Again he glanced down at his papers. 'Your war efforts in the European war zone did you proud and the entire US Army hold you in the very highest esteem.' He stood up and, looking at me, said, 'Now I really must tell you why I wanted this talk for it's about you being discharged.

'The American army works on a points system and you, my corporal, have well over the necessary number of points to be sent stateside, yet there is something else besides taking a discharge that I can offer you. You may have a long leave to the States and on your return will be made up to staff sergeant.' I had already made up my mind on hearing this proposal, for this would prevent me from seeing my wife and child, so I said how sorry I was but had to turn down the offer and leave the forces.

I was not sorry to leave the island of Okinawa and when about 200 of us got on the ship there wasn't a tear shed. I never could understand why the postal unit was sent here in the first place, for the amount of mail received and sent out to the States was very small.

Now it was time for our long trip back to the state of Washington. Again, as on all the other ships, it was the same old routine but I suppose not quite so severe, for I think the officer in charge knew we were all on our way home to be discharged.

Our time on the boat passed very slowly. Eventually, after breakfast one day, land was sighted. This particular place had been bombed and the harbour literally destroyed by the Japanese. It was the reason why the USA had declared war on Japan and Germany. We had arrived in Hawaii and Pearl Harbor.

There were gasps of surprise from the men on the ship as we docked in the harbour, for we were looking at an expanse of water that had dozens of big ships still sitting where the Japanese had bombed them. The upturned, rusted bottoms of some of the warships were all that was visible and it was a sorrowful sight. It was very sad to think of all the sailors who had lost their lives in this surprise attack.

The ship stopped at the harbour long enough to take delivery of fresh food and other necessities and so we were allowed to go ashore for a short spell. Hardly anything there had been repaired. Seeing all the damage there was, I had time to sit down and meditate.

But all this is only a part of my eventful life.

PART THREE:
A New Life in England

Coming Home

I got married at twenty-one to a lovely English woman and our son was born while I was still serving my time in the army, on the island of Okinawa. I was once told by a man that I had lived a charmed life. The sight of Pearl Harbor brought all these memories back and a lot more was yet to come. Only this time it was not about killing or bloodshed – it was all about being discharged and trying to forget the terrible past but I was sure my dreams would bring it all back. As the ship weighed anchor and sailed away from what drew the US into the war, I looked to the heavens and said, 'Bless them all,' for I knew how the survivors felt.

Days later in 1946, we saw the west coast of mainland America and soon the ship docked. If I could name all the battles and places I had to fight my way through on the map, then I'd have a memory of an elephant, especially as it was so long ago. I can only bring to mind that the port the ship arrived at was in Seattle, Washington, the furthest north-western state in the USA at that time.

The soldiers on my ship were taken to an army

camp. I can't remember its name but I can say the scenery was fantastic. In the distance we could see the mountains and giant redwood trees. I reckon the biggest surprise the men got was not the majestic outdoor beauty, but who was walking around inside the camp. It nearly made me sick with anger. Even today I still can't comprehend how it could happen, for before me were not the Americans I had expected to see but many German prisoners of war. I couldn't count the number I saw because there were so many everywhere.

What made me so damn mad was that I'd experienced hell fighting them, and now here they were POWs, living a life of relative luxury. When I'd joined the army to fight for my great country, I had no doubt in my mind that I could have died but still I didn't understand why a German was treated so well. I'll bet if the shoe was on the other foot we would have been treated far differently.

Anyway, ignore the fact that I felt as if I was abroad again because it didn't last very long, as the group of men I was with dispersed in different directions. This was after we were in camp for a few days. I believe this camp, barring the POWs, was the best one I'd been in for a long time and I knew I would miss it.

When I left the army camp with many more of the soldiers, we were sent off in style. We soldiers got on a variety of Pullman trains going to different destinations. The date was 8 January 1946 and my place of destination was Fort Devon, Massachusetts. This was where I was to be given my discharge. The days went by one after another and we got off the train every day for exercise. It was strange for me, as I knew full well that this journey was the end of my army life. I must admit if I hadn't married and had a son maybe, just maybe, I would have stopped in the forces, but not in the postal unit, for I felt I belonged in the infantry. All of my service life, barring my time in the postal unit I'd served in the ground forces in Europe.

I'd been in the 28th and the 8th Army and promotion was offered to me, but I felt I had to get to know my wife again and meet my son David for the first time. On 18 January 1946, I reached Fort Devon, to go through the very same ritual as we went through joining the forces, although this time I was getting out. First we had a good night's sleep after the long train journey, then the following morning I had to see the doctor to be pronounced physically fit for discharge. I was told I'd have to see another doctor because they weren't satisfied with my right hand.

This, of course, was due to my old injury, which I'd known about for months, and if they'd looked up my old army records they would have found out I had three dead fingers on my right hand. This was due to a bullet having shattered a bone in my wrist. I couldn't feel someone pressing my fingers. In fact, I could hold a lit cigarette between my trigger finger and the middle one and I wouldn't feel anything, although it would leave a blister between my fingers.

Quite a long time after, I was eventually passed,

with only this small disability, and I received my new uniform. At this time they asked me a question that puzzled me: 'What regiment would you like to be discharged from?' I could have picked any one, for, as I've stated before, I served in two infantry regiments and a non-combatant unit. So I chose the one I joined after my basic training and without hesitation said the 315th infantry division.

Why I chose it I will never know. Maybe I left the other one out because I wanted to forget the nightmares. Now with my new uniform (for they didn't offer civilian clothes), my few dollars and train ticket, not forgetting my honourable discharge papers, I left the forces on 20 January 1946; just seven days before my twenty-second birthday.

I caught a taxi to the railway station and, as I had quite a wait before the train's departure, I went into a saloon to have a beer. I leaned against the bar and asked the man serving for a pint. He looked me up and down and to my amazement he told me to take my uniform off, stop playing games and to come back when I was twenty-one. I was taken aback for a few moments and, before I realised it, I had a chair in my hands and was about to give him one of the best when someone held my arm. Another man stepped forward and the two of them held me to the floor. I was livid with frustration and I'm sure if I hadn't been caught in time I most certainly would have brained him. One of the many onlookers, seeing what was happening, picked up a paper that had fallen from my pockets; read it and handed it to the man beside him.

While all this was going on, I reckon half the police force in Boston had turned up. The paper was handed to a police officer as I was on the floor.

'Be God be glory,' said the Irish policeman, 'he's only come back from spending time in the war. Look at all these medals he's won.'

After that, believe me, those in the saloon couldn't do enough for me. Even though the bartender said how sorry he was, as he thought I'd looked too young to drink, I told him in so many words to stick his drinks and slammed the door after me.

While I was waiting on the station platform, I had a little smile, for I could see the funny side of this episode. Even to this day I keep thinking I haven't a grey hair on my head and I still look like a young boy after all I'd been through. Then, at long last, the train arrived, I collected my gear, got into the Pullman carriage and settled down for my long trip home. When I look back on my three years in the army and what I had seen and done, I realise that I went into the services as a green youth but I came out a grown man.

After a spell, the train pulled into Portland, Maine, and I waited patiently for a connection to take me to the town of Camden. While I waited, my mind went to the future because now I was a civilian again. What lay before me? I really think I was expecting a welcome-home celebration, when

I returned to my home town. When I stepped off the Greyhound Express, it was as if I had never left, for only shoppers and the locals were to be seen. I suppose this was partly because the temperature was twenty below zero and snow was lying everywhere. Well, it was the middle of winter and no one ventured too far in this weather, so my homecoming was not as I'd hoped.

I walked in my former serviceman's gear out to Nelsonville, five miles away. Good job I was fit, for even I was feeling the icy cold wind. What a welcome! It wasn't my parents' fault, for they didn't know when to expect me, but when I eventually went into my father's house it was like returning from hell to heaven. Nowhere would or could I receive so much love and I knew I was home. We had a reunion as such but I missed not having my son and wife to meet me.

I knew I had to wait for the army to send her to America as a GI bride. So in the meantime I had to get a job and get us a place to live. I went back to the old Seabright textile mill, to work in a large spinning room. I'd worked in a cloth-making factory before and my dad had worked in one for years. With the small army grant I got from the government, I learned the skill of spinning yarn on bobbins. It was a tedious job with little pay, but then beggars can't be choosers, so I tried hard to learn.

One makes mistakes in a lifetime and I made one of the biggest ones when it came to looking for a place for my wife and family to live. Instead of thinking what my lovely wife would want, I helped build a log cabin, just at the back of my dad's house. I, with the help of my brother Ralph, ran an electric wire from my father's house to the cabin and generally tidied the place up, hoping that she'd like it. Looking back I should have realised that wasn't right for a person who came from a city to live in an outside homestead. What I should have done was to rent a house until I could afford to buy some land to build a house on. This, at the end of the day, was one of the biggest mistakes I ever made and it was to change my whole way of life.

At long last, I got the message she was on a ship that was to land in New York on Saturday morning. I was elated, for I hadn't seen Joyce for thirteen months and had never laid eyes on my young son, whom we named David William.

With my best bib and tucker on – in those days in the States it wasn't a suit but just casual wear – I and my eldest brother, Vincent, who'd driven Greyhound buses before and knew New York very well, went to meet my wife and son. We slept overnight in a very old, cheap hotel. When I say cheap, we actually slept on the floor because the bed was crawling with bugs, but on the floor at least we were out of the cold. Morning came and Vincent and I waited outside the harbour barrier for what seemed like ages but it was only about half an hour.

Over the loudspeaker a voice said, 'Would the husband of Mrs Joyce Marion Nelson please report to emigrations.' Vincent and I hurried quickly, almost knocking over another ex-soldier, who was kissing and cuddling a woman I presumed to be his wife, and just a little way behind, there she was. We gazed at each other for quite a long moment. Finally, I held her and our son ever so gently as she wept.

As for young David, it was so wonderful to feel like a father and a husband rolled into one. I cannot remember how long we held each other but I got a slight touch from behind. It was Vincent wanting to meet his sister-in-law for the first time, and again there were tears of happiness. (I found out later that no GI bride could be let through the barriers unless she was met by her husband. There was a lot of unnecessary unhappiness, as many of the wives weren't met by their husbands. All those sad souls were taken to Ellis Island, either to wait or be sent back to England.) Without any more delay, we all got into the car to drive many a mile off to Nelsonville.

All the family accepted my wife with open arms and, being British, with her accent, she would be known for miles around. You can't live your marriage on a dream and maybe I was a dreamer. I went into the forces and learned how to fight for my life for three years, but didn't take seriously what a woman wanted in marriage. In the end, this would nearly be my downfall. My new English bride and baby son were welcomed into the family and she accepted them but we were all living too close, only about 500 yards from my father's house, and I suppose the different style of life didn't help.

She was from London and I was a country boy, as green as green could be. Every day I worked at the mill, six days a week, and of course Joyce was just left on her own to mind our son. There wasn't any television in those days so you had to make your own entertainment. I didn't want her to be bored but it was the same routine every day. I had plenty of conversation while at work, but poor Joyce was left at the cabin and I think, if it had not been for my brother's wife Arrabell, we would have moved back to England earlier.

My wife and Arrabell were the best of friends and they were always together. The two of them also got into the odd habit of waiting outside the textile mill every Friday at five o'clock and stand while Ralph and I threw our pay cheques out of the upstairs window. They both picked the paycheques up, and with my wife Joyce pushing David in a pram, they went down to Camden and waited by the grocer shop for us after work.

This went on for a year, maybe just a little bit longer, and all the time I knew she was getting very homesick but there was little I could do, for I hadn't the money to send her on holiday, in fact, we were as poor as church mice. How does anyone change their way of living if he or she doesn't have the financial backing? I was quite happy with all my brothers and sisters but Joyce was crying nearly every night and I knew that somehow something had to be done.

When I told my father about the problem he looked quite upset but said, 'Look here, my son, you've made your bed and must lie in it but please remember one thing: you raised your hand and gave a vow – now it's up to you how you keep it.'

Joyce must have written a letter to her mother about how unhappy she was, for a letter arrived one morning saying, if I wanted to, she would pay both our fares back to England and we could live with her until we got settled.

I was told my mother-in-law's son had also found me a place of work, for according to Scotland Yard (though it would now be the Home Office) I had to acquire a job and a place to live to reside in England. I thought many hours but then realised my poor dad had told me to do what was right and, as I didn't want to lose my wife and son, I accepted the offer but knew full well, as did my family, I was giving up part of my life.

Before I relate these changes in my life, I must tell of what happened about two weeks before we left for our journey to New York City, to board the ocean liner named *Queen Elizabeth*. My dad and I went for a long walk up Mountain Street, chatting about nearly everything and looking at the lovely scenery that fringed the bottom of Mount Betty, with trees of many kinds growing here and there. Just on the left of us was located Camden's cemetery, a huge one in which probably the oldest of the dead had been buried at least 200 years.

Dad took my hand and led me into the graveyard and we walked among the different-sized headstones. After awhile we stopped and looked down the hill. I could see the house in Sand Street where I was born. He then put his hand on my shoulder and said in a muffled tone, 'One day but only God knows, your mother and myself will lay here, so please remember this, son, and may the good Lord bless you and Joyce and my little grandson David.'

I will always remember my father saying this, for I'm sure he had a premonition he would never see us again.

This is another part of my story that I'll never forget. Although my father never went to church, he certainly was a God-fearing man and the tears in his eyes were something I'd never seen before. This part of my story must have been somewhere in 1948, maybe a little earlier, but what I do know is everyone in Camden had been told in the daily paper of the returning home of the GI bride Joyce Nelson, her American husband and their very young son David.

Everyone wished her well but the very ones to miss me and young David most would be my parents, for they had welcomed me back after the war and now, to their utter dismay, were losing me again. Only this time they were losing a daughter-in-law and grandson as well.

Very soon the time came for Vincent to take us away. This was too much for my mother. She cried so much that Dad had to hand David to Joyce sitting in the car. As the car pulled away, everyone was waving and I could see Arrabell wiping tears from her eyes. I'm sure she'd miss Joyce very much. Then we were on our way and had a long trip in front of us. Vincent drove quite a few hours and at long last we arrived at New York harbour. The four of us went to reception. This was where we all said goodbye to my brother and he waved to us as Joyce, David and I went up the gangplank and on to the great ocean liner.

The state room was nothing to speak about, in fact it was no different from the last time I had travelled in it except, of course, the last time there were canvas bunks and many hammocks. David really enjoyed the long trip across the Atlantic, even though the journey became quite rough, owing to the weather, but his little legs did him proud as he walked beside us. Four days later the liner docked at Southampton.

Going through customs took a while, mainly because my wife was still a British subject, so she went through one of the many gates and I another, for I was classed as just another alien. Later, the three of us boarded a train and it was a one-way ticket all the way to Waterloo Station. Our little son David slept nearly the whole way and I must admit both Joyce and I had long naps when we were not watching the scenery.

At last the train pulled into the terminus and we had arrived. We were extremely tired and Joyce's brother Reg met us as we came through the platform gates. Very gently he kissed his sister, for David was fast asleep in her arms. 'Hello, brother-in-law, how was the journey?'

I said, 'It was tiresome and rough but at long last we are here and it's nice to see one of my in-laws again.'

Getting into his car, the three of us fell into a deep sleep, as we travelled through London to his mother's house in East Dulwich.

Joyce was so excited she nearly tripped as she hurried to meet her mother. David was in my arms but, even as a very small boy, he was very eager to follow his mother, so I had to put him down. There stood mother and daughter having a good cry, with young David pulling at his mother's flowered skirt. Then when both of them were calm, he was raised up to have a cuddle with his English grandmother.

My wife's mum lived in a one-bedroom flat on the first floor of a council tenement. On each side of the landing, there was a staircase going up to the top floor with four flats on either side. There was no central heating but there was an open fireplace. Mum (as I called her) used coal, and sometimes railway sleepers, to keep the cold out. The coal and wood was usually kept in the bathtub, covered by a wide board. Every so often the fire in the hearth set the chimney on fire. To put it out, she kept was plenty of salt, and this usually did the trick.

I had to report to Scotland Yard to register that I had found a job. This had been arranged by my wife's brother. And the lodgings, well, the three of us were to stop with my wife's mother until permanent living quarters were found. I think the officials at the

Yard treated me very well. I showed them written proof about the job I had been given and where we were supposed to live. I had my photo taken and was then given a little book to identify me and my right to work and live over here.

My very first job was as a car mechanic, at Crossly Motors, Westminster, and my lodgings were as stated before they were with my mother-in-law at Cowdray House, East Dulwich. I believe I was only in the country two weeks before I started my first job.

I got on very well with all my workmates. I followed the very old saying 'when in Rome do as the Romans do' and so I did, and believe it or not, I was accepted as one of the crowd, even though I had a bloody American accent.

To get to the job at Crossly Motors, I had to ride on a tram and get very close to Victoria Station then walk down a long street to my workplace. The men who worked there welcomed me and helped me in every way. I think the Londoners were very friendly people and, looking back on my life in England I still think so. I am not bragging but I do believe that the work I performed was accepted as being top class. However, it became boring all day long taking truck engines apart and then servicing them, so, when the work dried up, being the last on the job, I was one of the first to leave and in a way I was not sorry.

I left this place of work with no misgivings, for no one was to blame. However, it put me in a spot for I had to find another job as soon as possible. Just down the road from us was a large building firm called Holland, Hannon and Cubit, so with cap in hand, I applied for a job and was hired the next day. I arrived at work the following day and the foreman met me and told me what they expected me to do: 'Stand six feet away from a lorry and catch bricks four at a time thrown to you and stack them up.'

What my workmates forgot to tell me was 'wear gloves'. This was my undoing, for as the hours went by, I looked at my hands and they were cut and bleeding all over. I couldn't go back the following day. I left the site, not only aching but really feeling down in the dumps. I had to go to the police station to report leaving the job but hoped to tell them I would be in work again soon.

With no money in my pocket and feeling depressed, I walked up a hill just outside our flat called Dog Kennel Hill. Down on the other side of the hill there was a place called Camberwell Green. It was here I passed a large hospital named King's College Hospital and thought to myself, shall I try for a job? It turned out to be the best thing I'd done since coming to England. Without hesitation they offered me a job as basement porter, one of the dirtiest jobs in the hospital. I grabbed it with open arms for this meant two things to me: work and money. I was to start my job the following day.

Before I relate anything about my job at King's College, I must tell you about the weather. Why? Let me explain. During my travels I thought I'd never see anything as bad as the winds on the Isle of Okinawa. I was wrong. In England it was the fog. The smog, as they used to call it, was so dense a person could put their hand before their face and not see it. All this smog occurred during the evening and cars were even abandoned. It was a nightmare. To travel, I just walked outside the flat and walked up the hill and down the other side to get to my place of work, but could only get there by guesswork. Only people who resided in London can know what it was like. Many people died, falling in the canal and drowning. How long this had gone on I didn't know, but I do know what it was like. The fog was caused by residents burning coal and so the smog came every night, while I was working at the hospital.

Anyway, back to my job at the hospital. As I stated before, it was the dirtiest job there. In the late forties there was no central heating in wards, so the only heat came from square hearths in the middle of every ward. The coal was collected from the underground cellars, put in a five-foot-long hand cart and delivered to each ward. This job had to be performed early in the morning, before any visitors were allowed to see the patients. It also had to be done twice more during the day and the evenings, or when needed. Other chores included the emptying of bins of anything that could be burned, for there was a small furnace just beside where the coal was stored. A basement porter's job had many tasks, not just cleaning. It was hard work, but a very interesting job. I had worked at this hospital for four years, when an accident happened at home.

My son David, who had turned five, was crossing the main road and was hit by a car. My wife was told by a neighbour and telephoned me at work. Dropping what I was doing, I rushed with my wife to the hospital at Dulwich. As it happened he was only bruised but the police told us later it could have been fatal.

David hated school as an infant and he had a very bad habit of going out the school gate and running down Dog Kennel Hill to reach home and I remember just how the school solved this problem. It was quite easy. They just closed and locked the large gates as soon as he went through them.

David was aged six when my wife became pregnant again. We were both very happy for David would have a brother or sister to grow up with. At work I was offered another job, a step up the ladder, if I wanted it. I was told later not one of the basement porters wanted it on two counts. The first was that it involved shift work in a forty-eight-hour week, and the second most important reason was because the job included taking the dead down to the morgue. I took the job.

The promotion I had taken was quite a rise above a basement porter, for now I became a casualty porter. I can also remember the pay was four pounds twelve and six a week. Overtime was not double pay but a day off for working it. For holidays, we received time and a half, but it all depended on the day of the holiday. I was issued with a uniform and cap to distinguish me from the other porters. Sister Doris was in charge of the casualty department.

She was a nice woman, but she certainly wore the trousers and we all did as we were told. Mind you, as it was shift work the two porters on duty were in charge most of the time, for Sister and the other women working in the office only worked weekdays. Not many people seem to realise that about the only type of disinfectant used at Kings in those days was Dettol. It was very rare for me to be examined by a doctor, so I was surprised to learn each patient was charged one shilling and having an X-ray was five shillings.

When all the staff had gone home it was our job to collect this money and give each new patient a ticket for every service rendered. The night shift went from eleven to seven o'clock in the morning and there was only one night porter on duty. The person who was on duty couldn't have a nap, for not only was he on watch but he also had to protect the casualty nurse. It wasn't as tiring as a day shift but could be very spooky at times. To me it was like going into an old church where many a person was laid out. I could always smell death, for I had carried a dead man on my shoulder in the war for a mile before I realised he had died, and I smelled it all my wartime life.

Walking down the corridors with a dull light wasn't so bad, but going up the ward with a boxed trolley to take a corpse to the morgue (with the help of another man) was very spooky. Then, of course, there was the hospital ghost, and if my memory serves me right we called him Ghouly. Once there was such occasion when I was talking to myself and a nurse tapped me on the shoulder during the night shift 'Bill, who do you think you're talking to or are you mad?'

Turning around, I said, 'I'm talking...' but there was no one in front of me. I felt like a nutcase, so kept on talking to myself and taking no notice of anyone close at hand. So what could I say but 'Well, I must be talking to myself,' and I carried on walking.

The smell of death? It gradually faded away.

I can't give the exact year, but while I was working in the hospital, the National Health Service was established. Two weeks before the NHS was to come into force, three doctors and I were having a chat. One of them gave his views.

'Listen to me,' he said, shaking a finger at us. 'Do you lot have any idea what will occur when this bill is passed? We'll have queues of people waiting at the door to be seen and be hard pressed to see all the patients in real pain.'

As it happened the doctor was right – queues were long but the biggest problem of all was trying to sort out the ones who had life-threatening problems. I was all for this change because it was free, but one and all wanted to get on the bandwagon. On day one I can remember two cases. One person had a splinter in a finger, a trivial thing, but then there was a serious case. A man came in feeling and looking extremely embarrassed. The pain on his pale face as he came close to the reception desk was plainly obvious. He moaned and clutched at something between his wide-open legs. He was moaning so much he became a priority case and went in the front of the queue. Everyone's ailments were considered private but in this case someone let it be known through the grapevine the patient had a thin curtain ring stuck around his penis and he couldn't remove it, because of the swelling. They didn't reveal how they got it off, but at long last when they did, to his extreme relief, it was the biggest laugh we'd had for a long time.

When David was six and beginning to like school, he had pains in his chest. The doctor was called and an X-ray showed he had a shadow over his lungs. The hospital suggested he go to St Mary's, a rest home for children in Broadstairs on the east coast; and so we duly took him at once. The home was run by nuns, and there were young boys and girls everywhere one looked. David tearfully kissed us goodbye and we left for our long trip home. Very sad. I can still see him waving his little hands at us as we went out through the gates.

Each week his mother and I visited him. A fortnight went by and his little body looked very fat and bloated. He certainly didn't look any better than the day we left him. I very kindly told the nuns we were going to take him home with us and much to their dismay we took him with us. Joyce and I, at the time, wondered if we hadn't been a bit hasty. It turned out a few weeks later that David looked his old self and the shadow, after he had another X-ray, had disappeared. So who was right?

A Growing Family

Time just seemed to fly by and in no time at all I had been working at Kings College Hospital for five years. Then my wife's labour pains started and because I worked at King's, she gave birth to my second son in the amenity ward, whom we named Terrence Nelson. Now we had two boys: a new born baby and another nearly seven years old. Joyce and I were very happy for we had wanted another child and David by now was used to school, so there was no longer any need to lock the school gates.

But in life there are always ups and downs and ours were no different. Everything was going fine at my work until I sneezed and there was blood in the phlegm, so an X-ray was required. The scan showed I had tuberculosis and I immediately went on sick leave and saw a consultant. A day later I was in and out of the out-patient clinic. The consultant, Mrs Simpson, was a woman I knew very well, for I had helped her many times, as I had most doctors at King's College and (even today I can say they were a wonderful lot). Mrs Simpson took a major part. She arranged for me to be admitted to a ward and the very next day I had an operation called a phrenic crush. This op involved crushing a cord in the neck, thus deflating my left lung. A few days after this minor surgery, I went home and waited two days before being sent to a sanatorium near Hastings. While resting at home I got very good news: the council had offered us tenancy of a flat at Number 13 Cowdray House, a flat just along the landing from my wife's mother.

My brother-in-law Reggie helped us move, for I was not yet capable of doing hard work. So the ambulance arrived one morning to drive me to a camp where I was to have total rest. I certainly was surprised, for my home had to be shared with another man. The structure we were in was the size of a beach hut. It had a roof but only three sides to it and the whole hut was on wheels. One or both of the men inside had to turn it to keep the winds and rain blowing into the open side. This was the only treatment that a TB patient could have, for there was no cure; the only treatment was rest and fresh air.

The month I had arrived here was November and from day one I reckon I did more outside work here than I would have done in any other job. Not real hard labour but pruning every damn rose bush and fruit tree in the fields of the sanatorium. I did this for nearly a month, and I've always thought I was released from this camp when there was no more pruning to be done. Anyway, I arrived home just a few days before Christmas and was greeted by my wife and David. My other son Terry was too young to realise my joy, but it was like an early present.

The return to work was a blessing in disguise, as the hospital only paid sick pay for two weeks, but something always turned up when least expected. Mrs Simpson, the hospital consultant of the medical team, sent a letter to the American Veterans' Department, telling them that I could have caught TB doing my spell in the army. The US government agreed, and I got a small pension from them, which certainly came in handy. Many people will think that, being a Yank, I must have received a big one. In fact, I only got it while I had the complaint, then it ceased.

At work everything was as normal and I carried on as I had left off, yet somehow things were not the same since the NHS came into force. Not that I didn't believe everyone should have free treatment if he or she had no money, but there were many who took liberties with the system. There are people who would take anything and everything free, even though they didn't need it. These people are usually the first in line to collect it.

I believe this was the lowest-paid job I ever had but can also say with hand on heart this was also the best, for there was never a dull moment, as anything could happen, and did. One day during the evening shift I went to Panta Rally ward to take a body down to the morgue. I was supposed to meet someone to help me to put the corpse in the cold vault. He wasn't there, so on my own I pulled the funeral cart to the mortuary. I very nearly had a heart attack, for although the morgue was dimly lit, I saw a figure in black leaning over a body on a table. No it wasn't a ghost, it was a rabbi, and the dead person was a Jew. This was their custom of staying all night with the dead. Now, you see, I learnt something new that night and these experiences will stay with me for ever. The staff of King's College Hospital treated me as an equal, for everyone knew full well where I was born as I still had my American accent.

There were occasions when I had to smile, for the red carpet was put out for the consultants and so on, but I will truthfully say I've never bowed to anyone since I came out of the forces. Mind you, I have the highest respect for a person having gone to the top in their vocation but then they're just human like me. In my jobs at King's, I believe there wasn't one person I disliked. Also, I did have the old-fashioned idea that nurses didn't do their work solely because of the money – they were dedicated to their nursing and were wonderful to work with.

King's College Hospital also had a private section for paying patients. They had their own porters and nursing staff, but it wasn't unknown for porters like me to perform a duty occasionally when they were short of staff. A porter here had to show willingness to do as bid. If he was rude or just talked out of turn he would be reported. I could understand why these private porters were different from the NHS staff for they relied a lot on the tips they received.

There are many people today who didn't know

how the system worked, before the NHS came into action. If a sick person was admitted into King's College Hospital as an in-patient, the almoner would pay them a visit. They would ask him about his income or if he could afford the treatment. If he or she had nothing it was free but if a person could pay just a very small percentage of the cost they would be expected to do so. I really believe this was a fair way of working.

At about this time, my sick pension from the US government was terminated because I was declared cured of TB. The extra bit of cash had made a big difference to our income and was very useful. I must say it also helped my family have some of the little extra things to live on. Don't run away with the notion it was a sizeable amount of money, as to be exact it was two pounds ten shillings a month. The English pound was at the time worth four dollars.

I had been working at King's for over five years and probably would have stopped there another five if Joyce and I hadn't received a letter from the council, offering us a house in Merstham, in the county of Surrey. There was a limited time for us to make up our minds for there were others on the list. I think having had TB was partially in my favour for everyone at the time was on the point system. I just knew without a shadow of a doubt, the job I loved would have to be given up. No way did I want to go by train back and forth to work, especially as I was doing shift work. But Joyce and

We made up our minds that it would be to our children's advantage, so I gave in my notice. David was seven and Terry was six months old when we packed our possessions into a van and travelled thirty miles to Delabole Road, Merstham. To all of my family it was paradise, a whole house all to ourselves, including back and front gardens. Mind you it took us hours to do all the alterations to the overgrown garden and make the inside of our home as we wanted it.

I still had to find a place of work. Before this, however, I had to travel to London to take a driving test. I was lucky and I passed it. So with my new driving licence, I bought an old banger and started to look for work.

As I had worked in a hospital, I looked around for one, near to where I lived. To my relief, there was a mental hospital at Hooly Lane about three miles from where we lived. This wasn't as large as King's College and more of a sanatorium where fifty per cent of all the inmates were behind locked doors. All the other patients were on the borderline of being insane. This wasn't a job for a porter but, as I'd been working as such, I was offered the job as an indoor postman.

The most important object I carried turned out to be a set of keys that opened up a large bedded ward, where a nurse on duty would take the day's mail, after which I'd leave, locking the door behind me. A person had to have his wits about him at all times, although some of the minor in-patients, the ones not locked in the dormitory, were allowed to walk the corridors.

There were a few times when I saw, to my utter astonishment, many unescorted patients who urinated against the walls. No wonder the cleaners were busy all day. It was OK for me to deliver letters and some times the odd parcel, but there was no way I could accept a letter to post. Time after time big parcels were delivered to the patients, either locked up or not. It was one hell of a job sending them back to where they came from.

Located just to the right of the building, there was a large brick enclosure, the fence around it at least six feet high. It was here where some of the locked-up inmates had their freedom to walk about, with supervision, but this was seldom done. I'm sure it became a treat to the not-too-mentally-ill patients, but I'm also pretty sure half of them didn't know what time of day it was.

Maybe this is the wrong time to stress this in my story, but I just must say everything I can remember. Neither I nor any of my brothers or sisters have been financially well off. It just seemed every one of the jobs offered to me was well underpaid but, like my own father, I wouldn't accept charity, so whatever the wages were, the bills my family owed were paid. One thing I definitely can say in my lifetime, we always had a holiday. How could we afford it? Well, one week's money paid for one week's holiday.

We always lived on a very small budget but got by on what we had after paying all the bills. As time went by my wages rose and instead of a caravan or tent, it was an all-in holiday camp at Butlins or Pontins.

Going on my postal round one day, I went up to the large barred door, unlocked it, went in and relocked it. The nurse in charge put her hands out to accept the mail, and as she did so I noticed two women. One was standing; the other was just behind her in a seat, but slouched over.

The young nurse dropped the mail as the first woman shouted, 'Why did you do it, you bitch?' and jumped on the other screaming insults. Then one started to pull the hair of the other.

'Give me a hand,' shouted the nurse and we rushed to where the two were fighting. We soon had them separated and the nurse put the one she held back into the chair and the other patient had a needle put into her arm, containing a sedative. I finally left this ward feeling very depressed. God knows what the young nurse felt like. In a way, she must have been pleased I had turned up when I did.

My work there wasn't always doom and gloom. I remember unlocking the door of another room and walking down the aisle and being confronted by a young woman of about thirty. She grabbed me around the waist and wouldn't let me go. This episode happened about eleven days after my ordeal with the other two women and therefore it made me feel a bit nervous of what the outcome would be. The head nurse was quickly on the scene and in no time at all she was talking ever so softly to the young patient. Then I was beckoned and she smiled. 'Ruth says she will not let you go without having a big kiss.' This was no problem, so I was let out of the locked door.

The not-too-dangerous inmates were permitted to walk wherever they liked. The hospital agreed on this because they weren't considered a threat, but I found out this was not totally true. Nethern Hospital was situated on top of a hill and the winding curved road to it started at the small town of Hooley. A railway bridge was at the bottom, about half a mile from a few shops. This was called Killer's Fall. While I delivered mail and worked at the mental establishment, there were no fewer than eighteen people who committed suicide by throwing themselves on the track in front of the trains.

One day, I was in conversation with a top medical doctor. Many subjects about the hospital and in-patients were brought up, though nothing personal; we were just passing the time of day. He then came out with something I should have known.

'Bill,' he said, and pointed at two patients. One was sitting in a chair having tea, the other was staring into space, 'take those two. The one sitting knows no other life yet is happy to be waited on at all times.' He paused and spoke again. 'The other woman is where she should be. I believe there are more of these people outside than in.' I believe he was dead right.

I had been working there less than a year when I learned that one had to be on the alert at all times. I walked by a male nurse who had quite a few of the borderline patients with him. They were all outside, digging a trench. As I went passed them I heard someone shout 'Don't do it!' and heard a 'thud' sound. Looking around I saw the male nurse on the ground and blood everywhere. He had been hit with a spade and the patient who held it was holding his head and crying. This had been a tragic mistake on the nurse's part, for he would be alive today if he had followed the rules to always keep your eyes open at all times and always be on the alert.

Not long after this tragedy, I had more of my own troubles. I was diagnosed with tuberculosis again. I have no idea why it came back. Maybe the cause was stress, for I had had quite a few nightmares of late and every night they seemed to be getting worse. I had worked there three years, and with a heavy heart, had to go on sick leave. I knew full well the sick pay would only last three weeks then it would be back to the labour exchange again.

The last day at work, just before leaving on the sick, I went to wish many of the patients I had known all the best. Then I gathered up my belongings to make my way to the head office. Looking around me I wished everyone good luck and then did as I was told and went home to bed.

There was a drug just available on the market called streptomycin. It was given to me by district nurses named Philips and Sheehan and the two of them took turns injecting me every day for a whole month. Believe me, my bum looked like a pincushion. I went through hell, for I had nothing to do and my mind played tricks on me. I do believe the drugs, and complete rest cured me of TB, but another month in bed, isolated from all my friends, would probably have sent me back to the mental hospital as a patient. Anyway, after the month had come to a close, the doctor sent me for an X-ray and I was declared fit.

The position as postman at the mental unit had been filled so with cap in hand I started to look for another job.

The name of the shop I was to work for next was called Forest Stores and I had a small red van for deliveries. I must say I can't remember the shop owner's names but I knew they were husband and wife and very nice people. I do reckon I must have driven at least 100 miles a week, so I got to know the territory like the back of my hand.

Nearly three years later, the boss's wife had just passed her driving test and I was asked to take her on my rounds for a week. I was stupid, for anyone with sense would have known his job was on the line. Two weeks later, the manager's wife had my job, so I was jobless once again. Now I had to look for another place of work. I'd never found it very hard in the past finding work but knew that one had to look for a job instead of signing up at the labour exchange.

At this time my wife was pregnant with our third child and the baby could be born any day. All the family were told the good news and that very evening we had a lovely meal to celebrate it. David was fifteen and Terry, seven. This meant there would be seven years between each one of my three children.

Two days I looked for a job, and at last I met a man I hardly knew. 'Have you tried for a job at Monotype near Salford? I hear they have vacancies,' he said. Thanking him, I immediately got into my car and drove to the place he mentioned.

I was interviewed by a bald man, who asked me all kinds of questions. At long last he was satisfied with all my answers and I was taken on as a security guard. They then measured me up for a uniform and I started on my shift the following day. This became a job of three shifts. All this entailed was standing at clocking-in points all over the big factory, but only during the night shift.

During daylight hours there were two gates to stand guard on. On both west gate and east gate no one was allowed inside Monotype without permission. Three weeks before Christmas, Paul, the works barber who did haircuts for the staff, started to do a raffle for Christmas. The top prize was two stuffed birds. To be able to win this, a ticket was sold, costing one shilling, but everyone was delighted with the prize and prospects of winning.

The raffle tickets sold really quickly, just like hot cakes, right up to two days before Christmas. The day before the Christmas holiday, the prize would be drawn. On this day I was just standing by the heavy wired gates, watching the day staff coming in and going out, and noticed Paul. He looked to be very much on edge and looked worried about something and he had every right to be. The draw was just about to take place and the staff not at work had gathered for the big occasion.

Everyone was in for a very big surprise: the number of the raffle ticket was called. The winner was an old man and he went forward to collect his prize. Everyone who was in the crowd cheered him and clapped their hands. Then the barber came forward.

'My fellow workmates,' he said, 'may I now present the prize you all had paid for,' and from a pail close by him he took out a square parcel to hand to the man.

Then with a look of disbelief on his face the man undid the parcel. There was complete silence as he did so, for in his hands were two trussed sparrows. Then the silence of the big crowd of people became one of laughter every one of them was holding his sides. This story did have a happy ending though. The man buying the raffle ticket had a return trip to Brighton, all bills paid.

The rest of the money was given to a charity. I do believe the barber got off lightly, for there were many who paid for the raffle who felt they had been cheated and it wouldn't have surprised me if all those people had given him a hard time. Anyway, maybe because the majority of them took it for a bit of fun they just backed down.

The following August everyone at home was very excited, for Joyce had given birth to our third baby, another son, whom we named Paul. He came into this world at 49 Delabole Road. He was the only one of my sons born at home, for David and Terry were both born in a maternity ward, in separate hospitals. My wife had complications in labour with all three, but our sons were healthy. Joyce and I had always wanted a daughter but we would not exchange our wonderful sons for all the money in this world, for they were and always will be our happiness.

I was on night shift when my wife gave birth, so had more or less all day to talk to my wife. After holding our son for a long time, she passed him to me. I placed him in the crib beside her and tiptoed out of the room. In no time at all she had dropped off into a deep sleep, for it had been a painful time for her with the stress involved.

That night, back at work, I had the first round to clock. This meant there were fifteen points halfway around the factory and fifteen on the return. In between each point there had to be checks made to make sure everything was OK. At one of these points, the large gate had to be opened, so a guard could enter the outside club house for inspection. Looking right and left I unlocked it and went inside. In the corner I saw the large three-pence slot machine and, just for the hell of it, I put my last three pence in and pulled the handle.

I turned around to make toward the door and heard a clattering of coins. They were all hitting the floor and then rolling by where I stood. I had hit the jackpot. Sure I was lucky, but how the hell could I explain this to my daytime bosses? There wasn't a great deal of time left for me to reach the next clocking point so, without delay, I got on my hands and knees and scooped up as many coins as I could, but had to play the machine once more to change the jackpot. At this time I thought to myself, 'What would the cleaners think when arriving the following day to see a load of three-pence pieces here and there on the floor?'

Making my way quickly out the door and locking the gate as I did so, I went to the next clocking point. I couldn't help but wonder – this was probably the only time I had hit the jackpot and only lost a few three-pence pieces.

My time at Monotype only lasted three years. There wasn't much of a prospect with this job and this probably became the reason why I left, to take an assistant manager's job at the Blue Star Garage in Redhill.

I never did get on with the job at Monotype. It may have been because I wasn't English born. Anyway, I suppose I was a little browned off with the work I was doing.

David was getting on with his education and, to get his pocket money, was working a few hours each week at the garage I was to take a job at. My wife and I couldn't afford to give him financial help, so this came with his part-time job. Every other way we were supporting him and he would soon be going on to further education. His mother and I were very proud of him.

He was a very lucky young man, for going to Redhill one day he felt his backside getting hot. He quickly put his motorcycle brakes on, falling, as he did, away from the bike. He was lucky, for the motorcycle was burning fiercely, and he was very fortunate to escape being burned or maimed. He picked himself up, went into the garage and called the fire service.

Shortly after this event we moved to a new address, 2 Huddleston Crescent. It was a three-bedroomed house, very close to the shops, with a lovely front and back garden. My wife's mother gave up her council flat in London to come and live with us and everything was falling into place. What more could we ask for?

By coincidence, I found myself returning to the same type of job I had been offered when I first came to this country. It was reassuring to know that someone had at last hired me for my knowledge of mechanics.

However, to my regret, as assistant manager, I was to learn that I would not be required to repair cars. There were the very rare occasions when I had a private repair job on a car and this gave me an extra income. David worked with me when he had spare time and there were days when he made quite a lot of extra money.

In this account I can't give any names of the staff because of the privacy involved. The manager did take lots of liberties, although he was one of the best men I knew. He had lots of outstanding problems as he loved wine, women and gambling. I wouldn't say he was a heavy betting man but there became times when the books didn't balance. Why was it, when this occurred, that there was always a break-in the night before the auditor arrived?

Remembering some of the details of the work is easy. I still think of the time a policeman, not in uniform, drove into the garage and pulled up at the pumps. We were very busy at this time so I asked the man to put in as much petrol as he wanted. I reckon he was at the pumps for five minutes, whistling as he stood there. Walking over to him, I took the hose from his hands and pointed at the front of the car. He looked in amazement at the petrol running beneath the wheels of his car and down the road. The rubber pipe running from the outside filler cap to the petrol tank had become dislodged, so instead of filling the tank it was running away. God, it must've taken at least two hours to clean up that spill. Anyway, we did clean it all up. As for the policeman, well, by the time he vacated the garage I think he was skint.

There were times in my job at the garage when mistakes were made and one I made was laughable. It was during the late shift and at the time it was quite dark. A man walked past the petrol pumps and came up to me.

'Excuse me' he said, 'Can anyone help me out? I've run out of petrol about a mile up the road.' Without hesitation I asked the other man working with me to take charge as I would not be too long. Filling up a one-gallon can, we were on our way to where the man's car had been abandoned. He had run out of petrol in a very deserted part of a country lane.

When the petrol had been put into the empty tank, he paid me and his car started first time. He waved goodbye as the vehicle drove out of sight. Another satisfied customer, I thought and got into my car, drove about fifty yards and ran out of petrol myself. At that moment I could have kicked myself up the arse for being so forgetful. Anyway, the damage had been done, so I started walking and as there were no street lights the walk took me what seemed like an hour!

Walking on to the forecourt of the garage, I was met by the manager. When I told him why it took so long to return to the garage, he went off in peels of laughter. I was so upset when I returned from picking up my own car that I damn near poked my fist down his throat.

Then there was the time that a very good customer of the garage bought himself an eighteen-foot sailboat. The main road went past our petrol station on a slight bend but there was a fork in the road, and our garage lay between the V-shape, with two roads passing us on either side. The man's name was Roy and he had just purchased this yacht and was taking it to his home in Croydon. The boat was being towed on a huge trailer and I would suppose he was travelling about thirty miles an hour. He glanced in our direction as he went by and I waved back but, in taking his eyes off the road for a second, Roy caused a stupid accident.

The car in front slowed down nearing the fork

and corner in the road. Everybody yelled, 'Oh no!' and the car that Roy was driving stopped. The momentum of the quick halt pushed the yacht off the trailer, carving a large 'V' into the top of his car. No one was hurt but there were tears shed by Roy.

There were times in this job when we had hardly a moment's rest. It seemed as if the evenings were more restful than the days. No one seemed to mind for the days seemed to go much quicker when there were a lot more customers about. Usually, there were two men, on duty, three if one counted the manager. Sometimes he was somewhere else, in which case I took on the job of manager.

In those days, the petrol was put into the cars by a full-time petrol-pump attendant and it was a must that he also checked the oil and tyre pressure. Having performed all these acts, more often than not, the driver would give him a tip. I always found it to be the driver who couldn't afford it who would do this and the old saying runs true, 'only the poor give to the poor'.

I was offered the chance of running a garage, to go into partnership and share the profits. Why I never took the chance I'll never know but the man offering me the deal was called Mr Moony. He often came into the garage on his way home to Hove, near Brighton. He always called me to do the odd job on his Rover and we got on very well. One evening he came in and asked me if I'd be interested in doing another job. This certainly could have changed my life but at that time I said I would think about it.

I should have accepted. I would have been expected to hire the staff for the garage and run it the way I wanted to. The profits would have been divided between the two of us and my wages would have depended on the amount of money made. Everything seemed to be above board and he said he would get all the legal papers drawn up by a solicitor the following night. I nearly accepted his offer. In fact, I should have said yes at once; I felt over the moon. I would most certainly have given two weeks' notice, but the garage manager was at home.

Moony drove away from Blue Star garage saying he'd see me at the weekend and I carried on working, hardly believing what a lucky man I was. Good job I never gave my notice, for the following evening my dream job was no more for bad luck came in the form of an accident. Mister Moony, driving on his way to Brighton, was involved in a freak accident and was taken to hospital where, on arrival, he was pronounced dead and all my dreams were no more.

Up to the day I'd been offered this job, I'd been at the garage three years and, in all that time, had really enjoyed my work. David was going to college and I was teaching him to drive.

I really found the customers interesting and many times helped them with their car problems but, after the accident with Mr Moony, everything seemed to go wrong. Not long after this disappointing news, more followed.

When the manager was found guilty of fraud

and sent to jail, I felt really sorry for him for he had always treated his staff very well and everyone respected him. We all knew about his bad gambling habits but this news came out of the blue. So I was told to take over the running of the station until the firm could nominate another manager. This really made me angry.

To put it bluntly, I had worked my arse off at the garage, ordering petrol, oil, tyres, and so on, and only did this because I had been offered the manager's job, but was truly let down by the management. Why did the firm let me down? If you were given the job of manager and were held responsible for a garage and did so for two months, what would your reaction be if it was offered to another person? The man to be put in charge had an uncle working at another local station and, to make it worse, he knew nothing about running a garage. I was then asked to teach him about reading the petrol pumps, ordering oil and tyres and so on. Now what would you do? I gave a week's notice and began looking for another job and, as for teaching the manager my job, no. I carried on putting petrol and oil in the customers' cars and would only perform what the other attendants were doing.

Not long after, I said goodbye to Blue Star. I found another job but not before the station had asked me why I was going. They even told me I'd receive a substantial rise if I taught the new manager in charge the basics. This angered me even more and I told them I had been treated better by the Germans and to poke their job. The position I'd applied for was half a mile from where I was working. It was an engineering firm called Foxboro Yoxall and it would take a whole book to describe what the firm made but, mainly, it was a stainless-steel object called a back-up plate.

I thought the best part of the job was the knowledge it was an American firm, though all the staff employed there were English. I must admit I knew nothing about factory work, although I had once worked at a cloth factory as a cotton-spinner. One thing was certain, I would do my level best to learn all of the trade secrets of being an engineer. The first month was the hardest but a pay rise was given to me after this time. If my work wasn't up to scratch, the firm would have fired me, so I knew that I had been accepted.

I was taught most of the skills of the machines from the lathes, to all the automatics and finally to end up on a big machine called a Borizer (used to widen a hole in metal) to a 1000th of an inch. Three months I worked on this job, and then finally I was given the chance to operate it on my own. The new machine was a lathe and this took quite a bit of skill for it was not a straightforward job. At first I did make a few mistakes but not long afterwards (after about a month) I mastered it.

The staff accepted me but there was always someone near at hand who would be making a quiet, snide remark and normally this would happen when an American visited the firm and started talking to me. Then, very close by, someone would say something offensive and nearly everyone would stand, smile but say nothing, pretending not to hear what was said.

I worked at this engineering factory for about two years before I was upgraded again, and to attain this I was never late and really worked hard at my job. Learning how to use all the large metal machines was a feat considering I didn't know anything about the shaping of all sorts of different metals.

The foreman was a good friend of mine and we had many a chat about different ways the job could be improved. As time went by, I did think of many ways to improve production. I think the foreman had put my name forward. However it happened, I became a grade-one setter overnight. After this real bit of luck, there was more to follow. Coming in the following morning, I made my way toward the foreman's room and he asked me to become the leading hand in charge of the back-up plate section. I was thrilled to bits for at last my hard work had paid off and the job was very challenging.

The section had a massive saw for cutting one-inch stainless steel discs from a seven-inch-diameter rod that was eight feet long. Also, the teeth of the blade had to be specially made from tungsten, which could cut through other metals. In fact, it was a specially built machine to cut through stainless steel and it took up a lot of space in the back-up plate system. The work was done by four men – a man on each machine, and with me in charge to make sure the items were made perfectly.

Many years I had been working in this country and I had found it's not what you know but who you know. The biggest boost was a worker being a freemason, for this you would automatically be a made man. I worked very hard in my job as a setter machinist and got to know the right people, so gradually I crept up the ladder until at last I became a grade-one leading hand setter. I was lucky, though even then, I was still aware of the sly remarks if I spoke to any visiting American, but as a rule they were far enough away not to be heard.

During my working years at this factory, I had a pain in my stomach, so went to see the local doctor. He barely looked at me and I was told it was just a bug that was going around, so I was just sent home. That night as I was going upstairs to bed, I felt as if something had just kicked me in the back, and I was just able to crawl up and collapsed on the bed. Joyce immediately called the doctor out, for there were no 999 calls then. He very quickly came and an ambulance was called for, as it was peritonitis, a burst appendix. I remember having an X-ray at Redhill General Hospital, and waiting for what seemed like hours before a local anaesthetist was found. I was wheeled down to the operating theatre and I remember the very last words I uttered as I had the needle put in me: 'thank God'.

I was told later the surgeon was a Mr Ede and he came from Australia. A very long time passed and I came around. Having worked at King's

College Hospital, I knew that they always put a patient just by the door, when he was very ill. I was put under so much damn anaesthetic and also having a blood transfusion. I knew as I got better they would put me further up the ward and nearer the recovery room.

They had me in this ward for two months, and every morning my bed was soaking wet, but every day I felt stronger and at long last I did end up in the recovery room. Then I had a relapse. The sister in charge of the ward was away on holiday and had forgotten to inform the staff nurse that I wasn't to drink more than a sip of water and so it's no surprise what happened. My wife and her sister came to visit and brought me in a bottle of Lucazade and, of course, I drank some.

God knows it was a terrible mistake for I was rushed back into the ward, heaving and trying to breathe. Luckily for me, the head ward doctor was close at hand and he tried his best to push a small pipe up my nose and into my stomach, but to no avail. I was nearly a goner. Then he tried to push it into my wide-open mouth and he succeeded, for all the fluid in my gut came back through the pipe and all over the bed, but at least I could breathe and I fell into a deep sleep.

I was in the hospital another month and to my utter horror found I had now inherited a very large stomach hernia and my God it was big. The hospital did not do anything about this, for the most important thing was the healing from the operation and the hernia could be seen to later. There was a fifty–fifty chance of survival. In the meantime, my wife had to go to work to help support the family, as money was again short but we tried our level best to keep the family together.

When at last I was able to come home, she did a night shift cleaning aircrafts at Gatwick airport. Quite a let down, from a shorthand typist to a night-shift airplane cleaner, but then we always loved each other and would do anything for our three sons.

I at last had the stomach operation for the mending of my hernia and, to the surgeon's disbelief, when they cut me open, he found my intestines had grown to the wall of the stomach. Again I pulled through and, looking back on the operation, the thing I remember most was the way the staff nurse tried to make me into a Christian. She tried so hard and forgot where she was supposed to put the saline drip. When I awoke the following morning, my right foot was twice the size of a football. I can smile about it now, but believe me I was a worried man. Did she convert me? Well, to tell the truth, I had already been converted because of the damn war.

In this story, I mention the regrets and tortures of my mind for what I have seen and done and in so doing maybe it will ease the pain of the past. I very rarely mention it, but even when I walk through the door of a cathedral, I can smell death and will nearly always think about the war. So why keep talking about it? This is probably a very good question and yet I have no answer. Maybe it relieves me to tell of what it was like to slay another man and, in later years, I still ask myself the same old question: if one of the old Commandments tells me 'thou shalt not kill', why was I put in the position at the age of twenty to do just that? So you see, I have a very long memory of trying to make sense of life and, until the day I pass on, I will still have horrible nightmares.

Epilogue

So after working sixteen years at Foxboro, I was given the chance to take redundancy. They all told me I was a fool to take it. It had been seventeen years since I'd gone back home to the States and in that time both my mum and dad and most of the family had passed away. I thought to myself, as I hadn't the money to return for the funerals, now was the time to go back, maybe for the last time, to at least see where they were buried. I took all of the redundancy and, with the spare cash, my wife and I went for the holiday that at last we could afford. I was in my fifties when I went and felt very sad that it was happening so late in my life. When we landed at Boston and caught the Greyhound Express to Camden, Maine, it was as if I had never left.

The mountains, lakes and scenery looked just the same but, when I at last stood over my parents' grave, where also my youngest sister Betty was buried, I went into a fit of crying and, looking up at the cloud-filled sky, wondered why.

I felt at the time that my life had always been in two places: my loved ones were in England and my other family was in the USA. The holiday was a huge success and I met around 230 relatives and about three quarters of them I had never met before. Then with a final kiss and a wave goodbye, we were on our way back to England.

I have in my army life earned a total of ten medals and ribbons and a citation for having made the D-Day landing on Omaha Beach. I also believe that every man who made this beachhead landing should receive the highest award available. That landing was one of the bloodiest battles in the history of war.

Life had its ups and downs but we could always rely on our parents to feed and clothe us. Food for our table would sometimes be scarce. There would not be much in the way of meat: the odd coney, squirrel or a deer would be a welcome treat. It was often the case for siblings to look out for each other. It clearly worked, for all of my kin managed to survive into adulthood. As there was no contraception in those days, large families were normal.

There were no televisions or computers in my young days. Our entertainment was sitting down and talking to each other. It always worked and still would.

I suppose the hard life our family went through helped us to mature faster than the offspring of the well off. And for that, I owe my parents a great deal, especially as war was on the horizon! We were told that the world would be a better place after the war. I sometimes wonder about that. I was never baptised but the war strengthened my belief in God, despite all the killing and slaughter we were subjected to.

I think that when children are given the Holy Bible, they should be encouraged to read and understand it, both at school and at home, so they may grow up knowing right from wrong. Britain is now a multicultural society and I now realise that schools teach children about other religions, to try to stem the tide of prejudice in the future.

I never intended to write this story about my life and the traumas I've experienced. Without the help and the questions asked of me by my grandchildren, this story would have remained untold.

> CPL Nelson 31220380
> 315 Infantry division
> USA Army